D0560323

To:_____

From:_____

Date:_____

A PARENT'S
BOOK OF
PRAYERS

A PARENT'S
BOOK OF
PRAYERS

DAY BY DAY DEVOTIONAL

TONY WOOD

B&H
PUBLISHING GROUP
NASHVILLE, TENNESSEE

978-1-4336-8324-4

Published by B&H Publishing Group
Nashville, Tennessee

Dewey Decimal Classification: 242.2
Subject Heading: PARENTS \ PRAYERS

1 2 3 4 5 6 7 8 · 18 17 16 15 14

Pour out your heart like water before the Lord's presence. Lift up your hands to Him for the lives of your children.

—Lamentations 2:19

No one can pray for your child better than you can.

No one knows their tendencies, habits, strengths, weaknesses . . . in short, no one knows their heart like you do. I believe the more specific we pray, the more specific we see our God respond.

I'm so grateful for the times when praying with others, their words have helped me speak what was already on my heart to say but I hadn't yet found a way to articulate.

In writing these prayers, in my mind's eye, I pictured myself sitting one-on-one with a wide number of family members, friends from church, friends from work, my own children, and even strangers. I hope these prayers lead you to pray for your child on a number of topics you might not have considered before. I hope they will lead you to lift them up with a degree of regularity you may not have before.

If these prayers have any value, at best they are simply jump starters. If on some days you find yourself only a sentence or two in and then you're off to the races on your own praying for your child—SUCCESS!

Thank you for allowing me the privilege of partnering with you in the holy pursuit of bringing your child before the throne of heaven.

May God be greatly glorified through the raising up of a godly generation.

Tony Wood

Thank You

TERRI—Of all the people on this planet, you're my favorite one.

LESLIE, MEREDITH, ERIN, AND JORDAN—I praise God continually for the privilege of getting to be your dad. I could not love each of you more or be more proud of how you live your life and how differently yet authentically you each walk with the Lord. Releasing this book is a really vulnerable thing for me. It's all the things I've been talking to God about, long before I ever saw you.

JUSTIN—There is no one else I know of that I would rather have as a son-in-law than you. I have prayed these things about you also from long before I ever met you, and you are God's answer to a number of my prayers.

CAROLINE AND PAIGE WOOD, AUSTIN AND VANCE ANDERSON, RYAN AND KYLE ANDERSON (nieces and nephews)—I love you all, and these are the things I've been talking to God about since you were born.

MARTY WHEELER (dad to Hannah), HOLLY ZABKA (mom to Jacob, Houston, and Violet), and DEVON DEVRIES (dad to Reegan and Rayf)—Getting this project out has been a *long* relay race, and each of you carried the baton for multiple laps before handing it off. I can't thank you enough for your friendship, belief, and partnership in ministry.

DAWN WOODS—Thank you for the door of creativity you opened to me. I will NEVER forget the moment you said, "Well, let me get my calendar and see when we can release it." My world shook! I was thrilled

. . . and terrified! Thank you for the opportunity, the friendship, and belief.

MARK HARRIS—This book would not exist if you had not walked into my writing room one day and said, "Hey, I want to write a song about praying for our kids and the dreams they dream." So grateful for that song . . . but more for the friendship.

ZACH OSWALD—One day I told my wife the joy was writing this book and the labor was typing it. It was killing me. The next week in the middle of writing a song, you leaned over and spoke "silhouette" into your Macbook. I had never seen "dictation" before. You changed my world that day!

Sons are a heritage from the LORD,
children a reward from him. – Psalm 127:3 NIV

My God,

I will never forget that moment when I first looked into the face of my precious child. It was the end of a long journey of wild anticipation. It was the beginning of another journey that is quite possibly the deepest, richest, most trying, and most rewarding one of my life.

Still today Father, as I consider Your goodness to me, I am overwhelmed with gratitude at the privilege of simply getting to be a parent. And with this great blessing comes great responsibility. I do not take it lightly.

Just as my child cries out when there is a need, hear me in this moment crying out that I need You. I need Your wisdom, I need Your strength, I need Your guidance. I want to be excellent at being a parent for my child. I realize my weakness, my inadequacy . . . and most of all, my need for You.

Will You fill me, guide me, use me, lead me today?

Amen.

For you are saved by grace through faith, and this is not from yourselves; it is God's gift. — Ephesians 2:8

Great Savior,

I will ask for many things on behalf of my children. I don't desire any request more than for them to have a saving relationship with You. No matter how deeply I long for this and no matter how passionately I request it for them, I can't make this happen. It only comes as a gift from You. Only You can turn a heart in repentance to You.

You have offered us the gift of Your grace through Your sacrificial death on the cross. Your Spirit is active in the world now calling hearts to come to You in faith. I pray that at a young age my children will hear Your Spirit calling to their heart, and they will be convicted of their sin and convinced that no one comes to the Father except through You. May they place their faith in You. May they trust You as their Savior and Lord. Jesus, not only is Your grace a gift, but the faith to believe in You is also a gift.

Will You give my child the gift of faith to trust in You?

Amen.

Protect me, God, for I take
refuge in You. – Psalm 16:1

Protector,

It would be unrealistic for me to ask that You keep my children from ever being hurt. Life in a fallen world means there will be bumps and bruises, cuts and scrapes. However, I do ask that You protect my children from serious harm to their body, mind, spirit, or emotions. Will You keep them so close in Your care that no plan formed to hurt them should ever prosper?

This is a world of so many dangers where news of accidents, disease, injuries, and evil are a daily part of life. This is a place as a parent I could grow fearful, but I will choose to take every thought captive and rest in the fact that whatever comes against us must first pass through You.

So Lord, wherever my children are, they are in Your hands. You are fully able to keep them safe and sheltered from harm. Will You please do that?

Amen.

I am Yahweh your God, who teaches you for your benefit,
who leads you in the way you should go. — Isaiah 48:17

God Who Is Perfect Truth,

I pray that even at a young age my children will have a special attraction to Your Word. May they somehow know deep within them that the Bible is like no other book in the world. May that interest bloom into a passionate desire to know the truth on those pages.

May they respect Your Word. May they want to know Your Word. But most of all, may they obey Your Word . . . trusting that You indeed are the Source of all true wisdom and that You can lead them into a better life than they can ever hope to have apart from You.

Even today Lord, would You increase their appetite for Scripture?

Amen.

A friend loves at all times.
– Proverbs 17:17

Jesus,

I pray that You would grant my children great discernment in choosing friends . . . especially in choosing who their best friends are. May there always be someone in every season of their life who is that one trusted and trustworthy confidant. May that be someone who also loves You and desires to walk in faith and wisdom. Will You give them a blessed and special relationship that brings much joy and happiness as they encourage one another to continue in ways that are holy and right?

I know along the way that there will be a number of friends who don't have a relationship with You. I ask that in these relationships You would allow my child to be strong, a good influence, and a leader.

May my children never be a "companion of fools" as Your Word warns, but may they indeed walk with the wise.

May they honor You with their choices and in return know Your rich blessings in this area of their life.

Amen.

Each person should examine his own work,
and then he will have a reason for boasting in himself alone,
and not in respect to someone else. — Galatians 6:4

True Judge of All Things,

From a young age my children, like everyone else, will begin to look around and compare themselves to others. It may be regarding appearance, intellect, achievements, abilities, possessions, or relationships. Though I wish they wouldn't, as they walk through a fallen world, they will.

Lord, I've seen how comparison can lead to pride, and I've seen how it can lead to shame and self-loathing . . . both dark shadow lands for the mind to roam. I have experienced how nothing destroys contentment like comparison. I pray that in the moments when my children are tempted to compare themselves, may they cry out to You for clear and right perspective. Would You meet them quickly in those moments with truth which will be light to drive back the darkness in their thinking? Will You return them to a place of finding their contentment in their relationship with You alone?

Amen.

What good is it for a man to gain the whole world,
yet forfeit his soul? — Mark 8:36 NIV

God Above All,

This is a loud world that will constantly bombard my children; trying to get them to concern themselves with things that are urgent, temporary, and ultimately insignificant. Many foolishly live all of life at this place and never turn their attention to the things that ultimately matter. I pray that my children will live looking beyond the plastic things that are momentary and focus instead on the real riches of what matters eternally.

I ask that my children will not be seduced into pursuing a life of ease, comfort, and acceptance by the world. Instead, may they see the wisdom of laying aside their own life and their fleshly desires for the sake of the gospel and Your kingdom. May they gladly wager their earthly life and their eternal life on the paradox that whoever wants to save their life will lose it and whoever loses their life for You and for the gospel will find it.

Amen.

How good and pleasant it is when brothers
live together in harmony! – Psalm 133:1

Father,

Some of the most influential relationships in anyone's life are those they have with their brothers and/or sisters. For my children I ask that their relationships might be deep, loving, tender, and cherished. May they be true and faithful companions as they travel with one another through the journey of life.

As we strive in these days to get to that place, misunderstandings, disagreements, and conflicts will continually arise. I pray that You will guide them to choose peace, love, and believing the best about one another. May they demonstrate grace and forgiveness and let no offense go untended or unresolved.

May they live so all can see that "family matters most." Will You guard, guide, and protect their relationship and ultimately use them in one another's lives as great relational training grounds for future relationships and also for the ways You will use them in serving You?

Amen.

Therefore, we may boldly say: The Lord is my helper;
I will not be afraid. What can man do to me?
— Hebrews 13:6

My Strength,

I ask today that my children will grow to display the quiet strength of character that is seen as confidence. Not a confidence in their own ability or anything that speaks of pride or arrogance but that calm assurance based on the certainty of who You are. May they be so sure of Your love in their life that it becomes a fortress wall against fear and stumbling blocks that come their way.

May their confidence also come from knowing how loved and cherished they are by their family. May this be another layer of solid stone foundation for them to stand on when facing trials and testing.

Even today Lord, will You move to plant this assurance deep into their heart?

Amen.

My son, if sinners entice you,
don't be persuaded. — Proverbs 1:10

Almighty,

Everyone has moments in life when a bad influence (sometimes from a good friend) will try to lead them into wrongdoing. My children will be no exception. Lord, I ask in those moments that my children will stand strong, choose to do the right thing , , , even if it means they must stand alone. Please give them strength of character to stand on their convictions of what is right and wrong.

May they resist the smooth words that entice them. May they recognize them as lies and press on in doing right.

May they know the blessing and joy of choosing to go Your way instead of going the way of the crowd. Please prepare them even now to make them ready for those moments when they come. May You be glorified in their choices.

Amen.

Love the LORD your God with all your heart, with all your soul, and with all your strength. — Deuteronomy 6:5

My Loving Savior,

As my children grow, the diamond of their character and personality will begin more and more to reveal itself. Just as every jewel has many facets that display different windows of beauty, so will their personality. Of all that You, I, or anyone else will see in my children, I ask that the most prominent and defining feature will be love for You.

God, I pray that my children's love for You will be fiery and passionate and encompass all areas of their life . . . their intellect, their emotions, their will, and their physical abilities.

May their love show itself primarily in a strong obedience to You and Your Word. May my children love the things You love and hate the things You hate. Even on this day, may that love show itself in their life.

Amen.

Do nothing out of rivalry or conceit,
but in humility consider others as more
important than yourselves. – Philippians 2:3

King Who Came as a Servant,

You were truly the ultimate example of a servant. You fully restrained all power that was Yours and took the most humble position in daily life (washing the feet of Your disciples) and in saving us (submitting to an unjust death on the cross).

I pray that my children will love You and desire to follow Your example. May they constantly strive to live with humility and to put to death any seeds of pride. May any evil seeds simply not take root or grow in the soil of my children's souls.

May they know success in the difficult battle of considering others as more important than themselves. May this play out in their relationships with other adults, with friends, and with siblings. May my children experience the deep joy, peace, and blessing that comes to those who desire to model Your humility.

Amen.

Let no one despise your youth; instead, you should be an example to the believers in speech, in conduct, in love, in faith, in purity. — 1 Timothy 4:12

Great Shepherd,

You know I desire for my children to be leaders and not followers. Any hope of them becoming leaders totally hinges on their character and the example they set. I pray they would set an example of goodness for others in the words they choose to speak.

I pray the overflow of their heart would always be something that is holy, pure, a blessing to You, and edifying to others. May their words be ones that are true. May their lips be free from crass humor, swearing, slander, demeaning and impure speech.

May love guide their language.

Amen.

The LORD is the One who will go before you.
He will be with you; He will not leave you or forsake you.
Do not be afraid or discouraged. – Deuteronomy 31:8

God Who Is Our Comforter,

Like everyone else, my children will have to deal with people who disappoint them, plans that fall apart, and desires that are thwarted. When these events happen, I pray You would send a good friend, a good song, or a passage from Your Word that reminds them how You are sovereign over all of their life. Remind them that You saw how this situation would play out ages ago. May this stir within them the confidence that You are leading their steps and that sometimes from our vantage point it may look like life is falling apart, but from Your throne it looks like life is falling in place.

Will You meet them not only with confidence, but may they find great comfort in the assurance of Your presence with them in the midst of their frustration? May they find peace in knowing You not only go before them but that You are close to them in every moment along the way . . . even in the darkest hours of their discouragement. May Your nearness be a dawning that restores their hope and peace.

Amen.

I the LORD do not change. — Malachi 3:6 NIV

Unchanging One,

You are immutable. You are the everlasting God with no beginning and no end. There was never a time when You were not, and there will never be a time when You will cease to be. There is never a change in who You are. You can never be any more perfect than You are or any less perfect than You are.

I pray that this truth about You will give my children great confidence in Your trustworthiness. As they live and grow in a world where everything physical is subject to change and ultimately proves to be unstable, may they find great strength and hope in believing that You do not and will never change.

May my children delight in knowing that Your plans are fixed, Your Word is sure, and Your will will be done.

Amen.

Godliness with contentment
is a great gain. — 1 Timothy 6:6

Our Sustainer,

You have made our hearts, and our hearts are only satisfied when they rest in You alone. Even I, an adult who is also Your child, sometimes I rest in You . . . and sometimes I do not.

I know my children will face this same struggle. I pray that You will keep them from the love of money. Though this is a world that esteems those who attain it, may my children hold to a different value system and long for a different kingdom. May they realize early that money is often like seawater—the more you drink, the thirstier you get.

May my children trust that You are sufficient for all of their needs. Would You guide them to know You as their faithful Provider? May contentment be a cloak around them that brings great peace to their days.

Amen.

Listen, my sons, to a father's discipline,
and pay attention so that you may gain understanding.
— Proverbs 4:1

Faithful One,

Many people declare their intent to follow after You. Some even start off strong but eventually abandon the narrow road of trust for an easier, less demanding, broad road.

I pray that my children will be found faithful to finishing the race that is before them. May their heart always be fully loyal to You, and may they be diligent in the pursuit of You.

May their example be so undeniable that it earns them the respect of those from all age groups.

Amen.

The LORD ... blesses the home of the righteous.
– Proverbs 3:33

Our Perfect Dwelling Place,

I think about the memories we are making these days among these windows and walls ... and the memories to come. Lord, a home is designed to be a safe harbor for hearts in a stormy, dangerous world. We want everything about our home to be pleasing to You.

May my children grow to love You more because of the time we will spend as a family in this place. May these rooms be seen as a place of grace, kindness, love, joy, peace ... everything that reflects Your presence.

We invite You to dwell mightily with us. Come fill these rooms.

Amen.

Pray constantly. – 1 Thessalonians 5:17

God Who Hears the Prayers of His Children,

May You often hear the voice of my children praying. I desire that they would learn that You are a God who longs for them to draw near and call on You. May my children be marked by the example of those around them that are faithful pray-ers.

Lord, would You have my children to be regular pray-ers, to have a time every day when they pour out their heart to You?

May they also be spontaneous and persistent . . . bringing all their concerns before You, knowing that You care. Would You have my children to be diligent intercessors on behalf of others? Even today, may their time with You be real and rich.

Amen.

Based on the gift each one has received,
use it to serve others, as good managers of
the varied grace of God. – 1Peter 4:10

Gracious Giver of Gifts,

I know every parent believes their children are uniquely talented. In light of Your Word and in a spiritual sense, I know that it is true of my children! Just as unique as their fingerprints, You have designed and wired them for special places of service in Your body. These are good works You have ordained from the beginning of time for them to do.

I pray that they discover what their gifts are and that they would be diligent to use them, being faithful in small things until You trust them with larger capacities of service. It will be my great joy to see the ways You plan to use my children's gifting for the benefit of Your church and for Your glory.

Amen.

I turned my thoughts to know, explore, and seek wisdom
and an explanation for things, and to know that wickedness
is stupidity and folly is madness. – Ecclesiastes 7:25

Holy One,

Evidence abounds that purity is not a virtue that is
esteemed or celebrated by this world. Yet in Your kingdom
it is clear evidence of those who belong to You.

Lord, will You guard my children's minds that the
impurities they encounter will not stick or become a
regular part of their thinking? Will You guard their heart
from the vices that would strive to take root? Would the
pattern of their lips be to speak things that are good, right,
and holy.

Would You impress upon them the high value and
incredible worth of sexual purity, and may they esteem it
as You do? In moments when they are tested in this area,
may they wisely flee from youthful lusts. May they serve
you with purity in all of their actions and intents.

Amen.

Encourage each other daily. — Hebrews 3:13

Encourager of Our Souls,

Some people are always pleasant to be around. Something about their demeanor radiates hope, kindness, and encouragement to others. I pray that my children will be among those people!

May it be that others somehow simply feel better about themselves from being around my children. May they always have something pleasant to say, and may their words leave others feeling cared for.

Since we never really know the difficulties those around us may be facing, would You have my children to be those who speak encouragement to others along the way?

Amen.

Forgive us our debts, as we also have
forgiven our debtors. — Matthew 6:12

Giver of Grace,

As children who are born in the aftermath of the fall,
we are all sinful and selfish and will naturally choose to go
our own way and not Yours. This sin of prideful rebellion
is our greatest weakness and the biggest problem we all
face.

I pray that as soon as possible my children would
comprehend the offer of Your incredible grace and cry out
for You to forgive their sin. I know You will meet them
in that moment with Your mercy and free them from the
ultimate penalty of sin.

Though this will bring them to be in the right
relationship with You, still like everyone else, they will
daily fall short and need Your cleansing. May my children
be faithful to cry out for Your forgiveness for the daily
offenses of their lives. May they know the sweet relief of
Your pardon. In response, may they live with great grace
for those who offend them.

Amen.

Therefore, since we also have such a large cloud
of witnesses surrounding us, let us lay aside every weight
and the sin that so easily ensnares us. – Hebrews 12:1

Christ Who Set Us Free,

Lord, I have seen how, though small and insignificant, a snowball can roll down a hill and pick up a great amount of mass and weight. I'm aware that along the way my children will pick up habits and ways of thinking and doing things. Some will be really good and useful.

At other times these small habits that are not good can grow as seasons pass and lead to harder consequences down the line. They can evolve into things that could hinder my children's walk with You.

Would You give me insight into recognizing these early on, and would You allow my children to have a tender spirit toward making changes that would help them avoid being entangled in unwise habits? May they run the race of faith unencumbered and with great endurance.

Amen.

The one who walks with the wise
will become wise, but a companion of fools
will suffer harm. — Proverbs 13:20

Faithful Friend,

You have made clear in Your Word, and I have seen it happen in life that those we associate with have power to shape our character. I pray that You will in all seasons of life surround my children with wise, like-minded, like-hearted friends. May the result of this be for both of them to learn great things from the other and be encouraged to continue in doing what is right.

What a joy for a parent's heart to see their children growing wiser because of the people they choose to be around.

May my children's friends bring out the best that is already in my children and even add good virtues to the ones that are already there.

Amen.

Seek first the kingdom of God and His righteousness, and all these things will be provided for you. – Matthew 6:33

King of Kings,

These brains You have created within us are wondrous things. Even in times of resting, we are running down a hundred alleyways of thought. There is always something on our mind.

I pray that the chief concern of my children will be for You, Your glory, and Your kingdom. This will always lead to right perspective in so many situations and help establish priorities. May it always be a place of sweet contentment and rest.

Will You guard them from having an obsessive focus on lesser things . . . food, clothing, and other pleasures, but instead may they set their hope and expectation on the eternal? This would be a harbor safe from fear and worry. For Your high honor, our King.

Amen.

Everyone must be quick to hear, slow to speak,
and slow to anger. — James 1:19

Voice of Truth,

You are always speaking. Your Word is waiting for us anytime we want to know Your heart and mind. I pray that my children will be driven into Your Word by all the events of life . . . the best and the worst. I ask that they will always want to know Your perspective.

In a world that values instant reactions to whatever newsworthy event is happening, I pray that in all situations my children's response would be careful and measured . . . given only after thoughtful consideration of what Your Holy Word says.

May this cautious response also guard them from premature expressions of anger.

Amen.

Reject foolish and ignorant disputes, knowing
that they breed quarrels. — 2 Timothy 2:23

God of Peace,

My children will sometimes be around friends and
others who obsess about petty things. They will attempt
to draw my children into foolish and unproductive
speculations.

I ask that You would guide them with discernment
in these moments, and may they be willing simply not
to weigh in. May they instead recognize these fruitless
discussions for what they are . . . and know that they
always lead to more quarreling and divisiveness.

May my children be at peace with simply walking
away.

Amen.

If you love Me, you will keep
My commands. — John 14:15

Most High God,

You know the desire of my heart is for my children to lead a blessed life. I believe this only comes from following after You. I want to see my children obeying all You have commanded in Your Word. Yet I'm aware that some people give an exterior appearance of obedience while simply masking a heart that desires to do otherwise. God, may this never be so with my children!

May their obedience come from a deep, passionate love for You and cause the riches of heaven to overflow into their earthly days.

May my children call You Lord and gladly do what You say.

Amen.

Go to the ant, you slacker! Observe its ways and become wise. Without leader, administrator, or ruler, it prepares its provisions in summer; it gathers its food during harvest.
– Proverbs 6:6–8

Ever-Working God,

Warnings against laziness abound in Your Word. It is a sure sign of disobedience to You and a disappointment to any parent.

God, I ask that Your Spirit and Your wisdom stir deep within my children. May they be evident through my children's self-motivation. Would my children have vision for all areas of their life and do great things on their own initiative?

May this be evident in schoolwork and learning. May it show in their approach to chores and work around the home. Particularly, may they be self-motivated regarding spiritual pursuits.

Would they, without outside influences, regularly spend time in Your Word and in prayer?

Amen.

As for me and my family,
we will worship Yahweh. – Joshua 24:15

One True God,

Oh ageless King who reigns on heaven's throne, I look around and see so many people have allowed something other than You to rule from the throne of their life. Regarding my household, we have made a choice . . . we love, serve, and live for You alone.

I pray that my children will see clearly the wisdom and blessing of this choice and in response will desire the same relationship with You. May they stand against the culture they will face and make the same bold declaration of belonging to You.

You are worthy of our trust and allegiance.

Amen.

Be angry and do not sin. Don't let the sun go down on your anger, and don't give the Devil an opportunity. — Ephesians 4:26–27

God of Joy and Justice,

Many times in my children's lives situations will cause them to become angry. I pray that they will exercise the fruit of self-control and not respond in a hasty, unwise, and immature manner.

May they never allow their anger to go unchecked, unacknowledged, or to linger in their heart. May it never turn to bitterness, resentment, or self-righteousness.

Would You always prompt them to seek reconciliation with You and with those who have wronged them? May they always be tender to Your Spirit's leading.

Amen.

And I pray this: that your love will keep on growing in
knowledge and every kind of discernment, so that you
can approve the things that are superior and can
be pure and blameless. — Philippians 1:9–10.

All Wise One,

There will always be some new spiritual trend or fad
coming down the road. While they pretend to be new,
most are really just a fresh coat of paint on some old half-
truth or lie.

I pray that my children's discernment will be such
that they can recognize ideas that are in tension with
Your revealed Word. May they never give time and
consideration to any works-based religion but always only
trust in the salvation that comes through faith in Your
atoning death alone.

May their discernment simply be an expression of
the overflow of their love for Your Word.

Amen.

Give, and it will be given to you; a good measure—pressed
down, shaken together, and running over—will be poured
into your lap. For with the measure you use, it will be
measured back to you. — Luke 6:38

Generous Giver of Grace and All Blessings,

You know the desire of my heart is for every good
blessing to come to my children. Just as I desire You to be
generous with them, I want them to demonstrate their
ability to handle Your blessings by being generous with
other people.

May their heart be moved by real needs, and may
they not simply feel deeply and then do nothing, but may
they take action and respond.

May my children be lavish in giving of their time,
talents, and treasures to You and to others.

Amen.

When pride comes, disgrace follows,
but with humility comes wisdom. – Proverbs 11:2

Pure and Perfect One,

My children will learn some lessons the hard way. There are others that, if they are wise, they will learn from observing the mistakes that people around them make. I pray that they will learn the lesson of how disgrace comes to the proud from watching others and that they will not have to experience it for themselves.

Pride happens on so many levels, great and small, but stumbling is the consistent result for those who persist in arrogance.

I pray that my children, because of their humble hearts, will be kept from being severely disciplined by You and being disgraced before others.

Amen.

If you keep My commands you will remain in My love,
just as I have kept My Father's commands and remain
in His love. I have spoken these things to you so that
My joy may be in you and your joy may be complete.
~ John 15:10–11

My Lord,

You invite us to know intimacy with You. As You
continue to teach us new depths of truth in Your Word,
we marvel at Your wisdom, Your grace, Your goodness,
and the beauty of Your gospel. Because we trust You and
love You, we want to obey You. As we obey You, we are
filled with joy.

I desire for my children to be filled with this joy. May
they find it by walking closely with You. Through their
obedience may they know intimate fellowship with You,
which always results in the fullness of joy.

Amen.

A man who endures trials is blessed,
because when he passes the test he will receive the crown
of life that God has promised to those who love Him.
– James 1:12

Almighty Giver of Strength,

At some point my children will begin to deal with difficult relationships. These may be in the neighborhood or in a classroom. They may be from someone who dislikes or picks on them. It may be from someone their age, or it may even be a strained relationship with a teacher or a coach.

In that time, Lord, help my children endure well. May they respond with self-control to hurtful words that are spoken. May they trust that You are the God who sees and understands all things rightly. As much as it is up to them, may they pursue peace.

Would You over time help them see the blessed reward that is theirs for enduring well?

Amen.

Children, obey your parents as you would the Lord, because
this is right. Honor your father and mother, which is the
first commandment with a promise, so that it may go well
with you and that you may have a long life in the land.
—Ephesians 6:1–3

Our Father Who Is in Heaven,

In today's verse I see two commands—obey and
honor. These two are so intimately linked. Obedience
refers to outward action. Honor refers to the inward heart
attitude of desiring to do what is right in the first place.

May my children never be outwardly compliant but
inwardly prideful or resentful. May they instead choose
to honor their parents because they trust You and the
wisdom of the pattern of "authority and submission"
which You have ordained.

May the attitude of submission and respect be a
strong foundation that sets them up for success in other
relationships that require "authority and submission."
Because of my children's hearts of honor, may they know
blessings in the quality and quantity of their life.

Amen.

The fruit of the Spirit is love. – Galatians 5:22

Loving Savior,

The greatest evidence of Your dwelling in someone's life is that love flows from them. We see how Your love was not simply good intentions and warm emotion, but it was always active in doing whatever was best for someone else.

I pray that even today the fruit of love would be evident in my children's lives. May it show in their relationships. May it spill over in their words. May it be clear, compelling, undeniable, and beautiful.

Amen.

But those who hope in the LORD will renew their strength.
They will soar on wings like eagles; they will run and not
grow weary, they will walk and not be faint.
— Isaiah 40:31 NIV

Our Rock,

Sometimes in my children's lives faith will look like standing still and doing nothing. This is always extremely hard! They may be tempted to run ahead of Your plan for them.

They may be required to remain where they are until the time You open a doorway or tell them to move toward the next place You are leading them.

Will You help them at these times to know the great wisdom found in simply being patient and trusting You? In those times of trial, may they indeed find that You are the One who at the perfect time will renew them with fresh strength for what they are called to face.

May Your faithfulness be their great hope in the waiting.

Amen.

Do not be conformed
to this age. — Romans 12:2

Holy One,

My children, long before they can ever recognize or articulate what it is, will feel the pressure of this world trying to squeeze them into the mold of whatever is worldly and current.

Instead of things that are timely, would You lead them to grow to love what is timeless? May they resist being shaped by the spirit of this age.

May they seek Your Spirit's leading in all areas related to fashion, entertainment, and language. May they seek Your heart and Your values.

Amen.

"Do not come closer," He said. "Remove the sandals
from your feet, for the place where you are standing
is holy ground." – Exodus 3:5

God of Abraham, Isaac, and Jacob,

I come today asking that my children will truly have a
spirit of reverence in all things regarding You. May a sense
of Your sovereignty and holiness affect how they approach
You in prayer and in worship. May it clearly color how
they speak of You always.

Please let them never draw near to You, in public or
in private, in ways that would be flippant or disrespectful.

May they at times know Your awesome presence in
such a powerful way that it leads them to tremble before
You. May a holy fear, respect, and reverence capture their
heart.

Amen.

Therefore, God's chosen ones, holy and loved,
put on heartfelt compassion, kindness, humility,
gentleness, and patience. — Colossians 3:12

Our Patient Shepherd,

We bless You for the way You are so merciful in dealing with us. If not for Your patient endurance with us, no one would ever be saved.

I pray that my children will exhibit patience like You do, especially in dealing with difficult relationships. May they find peace in Your sovereignty knowing that You see all moments they spend with those who are hard to deal with. May they trust that You know their heart. May they learn to sit quietly in Your presence even in the waiting.

May their choice of patience keep them from despair and from wrongly taking matters into their own hands.

Amen.

The poor in spirit are blessed, for the kingdom
of heaven is theirs. — Matthew 5:3

God Who Hears the Cry of the Humble,

I pray that from a young age my children will be
sensitive to the gospel. May they easily believe and agree
that all have sinned. In light of who You are, may they see
themselves as lost, helpless, and hopeless apart from Your
grace.

Would You help them see themselves as a soul that is
bankrupt before You . . . truly "poor in spirit"? May they, in
an absence of pride and with no way of saving themselves,
cry out to You for mercy and salvation.

In giving up their own kingdom, may they receive
Yours.

Amen.

I am a friend to all who fear You,
to those who keep Your precepts. – Psalm 119:63

Faithful Friend,

I come to You on this day particularly to lift up my children, asking that You would bless them with friends of the opposite sex. I pray that these friendships would be pure and holy and pleasing to You.

In a world that so promotes romantic relationships, I ask that my children would be able to resist the pressure of prematurely entering into relationships with those of the opposite sex. May they instead simply enjoy rich and rewarding friendships until the time that you lead them into a deeper, more mature, age appropriate relationship.

Amen.

Before a word is on my tongue, you know
all about it, LORD. — Psalm 139:4

All Knowing One,

You are omniscient. You know everything that has ever happened, everything that will happen, every possibility, every detail of every life on earth as well as in heaven and in hell. Nothing good or bad is hidden from You or goes unknown by You.

I pray that this truth will be revealed from Your Word and will leave my children amazed. May it mark them with great comfort that You already intimately know them and all their deeds, thoughts, weaknesses, and struggles. May this, coupled with the fact of how You deeply love them, lead them into greater worship and wonder.

May Your omniscience give my children great peace as well as be a sobering reality that they can never truly hide anything from You.

Amen.

All Scripture is inspired by God and is profitable for teaching, for rebuking, for correcting, for training in righteousness, so that the man of God may be complete, equipped for every good work. — 2 Timothy 3:16–17

Word of God,

I pray that even from a young age my children will experience a special attraction to and respect for Your Word.

Through all of life, may they trust Your Word to be sufficient for speaking truth into all areas of their life. May it be a guide for how to be in right relationship with You and with others. May it lead them in making good decisions. May it challenge and set before them a path of life that leads to incredible blessing. May it speak correction to them regarding any false doctrine they encounter or any sinful behaviors they commit. May it prepare them for every good work You have in store for them to do and help them discern Your will for their life.

Would You lead my children to look at all areas of their lives through the lens of Your Word? However much they saturate their mind and heart with it, may they always desire more.

Amen.

May integrity and what is right watch over me,
for I wait for You.   Psalm 25:21

Sustainer of the Upright,

Because of other people they associate with, a cloud of suspicion may sometimes fall on my children. Perhaps some wrong deed will be done by a friend of theirs, or they may simply find themselves in the wrong place at the wrong time . . . I wish that it would not happen, but I know that it will.

In those moments, Lord, may my children's good name and reputation come shining through. May they guard their reputation because of how it reflects on their family but mostly because of how it reflects on You.

May they find peace and rest in times of being falsely accused, knowing that You always know the truth.

Amen.

Therefore, whether you eat or drink, or whatever you do, do everything for God's glory. — 1 Corinthians 10:31

Worthy One,

I pray that my children will be passionate about Your receiving glory. May they want You to be glorified in their every decision and every choice in life. May they seek your leading and Your will for all relationships and areas of their life.

Even in mundane, routine, and seemingly nonspiritual areas of life like eating and drinking, may they seek Your direction. May they make wise and healthy food choices. May they choose to refrain from excess. God, will You keep them free from any addiction so they may not be hindered in serving You? May their life bear much fruit and bring You much glory.

Amen.

A person's insight gives him patience, and his virtue is to overlook an offense. – Proverbs 19:11

Gracious King,

I pray that Your grace will permeate the lives of my children. May it be so evident in them that little offenses along the way will simply roll off their back without being given much thought.

Would You guide my children to truly be slow to anger and quick to overlook the ways they have been offended?

May they not carry with them remembrances of past wrongs. Would You also allow their forgiveness to bring a sweet forgetfulness of the times when they were wronged? May they live free from the bondage of unforgiveness.

Amen.

Show proper respect
to everyone. – I Peter 2:17 NIV

God of Honor,

I pray that my children will be known for displaying good manners. In a time when disrespect seems the norm on so many fronts, I ask that my children will take to heart Your call for us to treat others with respect.

May it clearly show in the way they treat all in authority over them—parents, teachers, pastors, police, military and governmental leaders, as well as the elderly.

I ask that it will come from a heart that sees the value and worth of all people You have created.

Amen.

"For I know the plans I have for you"—this is the LORD's
declaration—"plans for your welfare, not for disaster,
to give you a future and a hope." – Jeremiah 29:11

Wonderful Counselor,

My children, on their own, could dream big dreams
for their lives. I pray they won't do that. Instead, may they
seek Your big dreams for their lives.

May they believe You have uniquely gifted them for
some areas of service. May they try different things along
the way that help them clarify and grow in confidence
with their gifting.

May they be willing to lay down all of their own
dreams on the altar of sacrifice. Through this will You
help them see clearly the ones that are from You?

May they know the great hope and the future You
have for them in Your plans.

Amen.

A good person obtains favor from the LORD,
but He condemns a man who schemes. – Proverbs 12:2

Friend of Sinners,

Every kid somewhere along the line will for a season
know someone who is that "Eddie Haskell" type of kid.
Parents can never quite put their finger on why they don't
trust that child, but it is a suspicion that is well earned.

I pray in those moments, Lord, that my children will
not allow themselves to get too close to the other child.
Will they respond to that check in their spirit and simply
not be attracted to that person.

It may take a while sometimes, but children like that
will always get exposed for who they are and for their lack
of character and trustworthiness. May my children learn
great lessons and wisdom from the consequences they see
fall on another.

Amen.

No temptation has overtaken you except what is common to humanity. God is faithful, and He will not allow you to be tempted beyond what you are able, but with the temptation He will also provide a way of escape so that you are able to bear it. — 1 Corinthians 10:13

Our Strength and Help in Times of Need,

I know that You will not tempt my children. You will, however, send trials their way. These trials will be times of testing and will actually be opportunities for them to give evidence of their faith and trust in You.

If they are not quick in declaring their dependence on You, it can open a door for the enemy to slip in and truly tempt them with something that would be an opportunity for failure.

I pray that my children will determine to go through every time of testing and use it to give evidence that they fully trust You, Your promises, and Your Word. May they cry out to You and find that You run to meet them, give them strength, and lead them through. May they repeatedly stand on the other side of a trial and give You glory for Your goodness and faithfulness.

Amen.

Be compassionate and humble, not paying back
evil for evil or insult for insult but, on the contrary,
giving a blessing, since you were called for this,
so that you can inherit a blessing. — 1 Peter 3:9

God of Grace and Glory,

We will never bear an offense or insult that compares
to the offense You suffered in being rejected by sinful
man. Even in Your death we see You speaking words of
forgiveness to the soldiers who nailed You to the cross.

I pray that when my children are mistreated, they
will not seek to retaliate. May they instead trust You as the
one who judges all people and events perfectly.

I pray that instead of seeking to hurt in return, they
will choose to bless. May they first bless their offender by
forgiving them and then bless them by praying for their
spiritual condition..

Amen.

Fathers, don't stir up anger in your children,
but bring them up in the training and instruction
of the Lord. – Ephesians 6:4

Holy Father,

You are always perfect in all the ways You deal with
Your children. I want to reflect You in the way I parent.

Would You please give me wisdom and guide me
to be firm, fair, and consistent in all the ways I train and
discipline my children?

I do not want to exasperate them. I know one
of the most common ways a parent can do this is by
overprotecting their children. Help me remember that I
am raising my children to release them into the world. May
I give them reasonable freedom to make their own choices
and even to make mistakes they can learn from. Would
You guide them to show maturity and responsibility in
these moments? May I not smother and hover so that my
children's spirits would become resentful.

Amen.

When I am afraid, I will trust in You. In God,
whose word I praise, in God I trust; I will not fear.
What can man do to me? — Psalm 56:3–4

Our Refuge,

This world is a frightening place. Yet so often in Your
Word Your followers are commanded to "fear not."

My children will feel fear and will need to make
decisions about how to respond appropriately in difficult
situations. Would You always meet them in that moment
with wisdom and discernment?

At other times they may feel the emotional rush of
fear wash over them, and it is simply an attempt of the
enemy to mislead them and cause them to question Your
faithfulness, goodness, or trustworthiness. In those times
may they make the choice to have confidence in who You
are and who You have revealed Yourself to be.

May they regularly experience their faith conquering
their fear.

Amen.

The body is not for sexual immorality but for the Lord,
and the Lord for the body. — 1 Corinthians 6:13

Our Provider,

I pray that through Your Word my children will have
a godly view of sex. May they correctly understand that
You created it, blessed it, and are greatly pro-sex in the
context of marriage.

Because of their understanding of it, may they desire
the best You have for them. May they choose to abstain
from sex until marriage. May they continually make wise
decisions to guard their eyes, ears, and mind from media
that would advocate and encourage a lack of self-control.

May the pain, shame, and consequences of sex outside
of marriage be a hurt my children never experience.

Even today I lift up their future mate, asking that
You put the same hedge of protection around them.

Amen.

Jesus Christ is the same yesterday,
today, and forever. — Hebrews 13:8

Unchanging One,

Our greatest hope and comfort is always found in Your character. As my children mature, they will become aware that they were born into a world that is in constant change. Because of the fall, change is rarely for the good.

They will see a planet in change—earthquakes, tornadoes, floods, fires; nations that are in change—war, political uprisings; and people in change—disease, death.

I pray that Your unchanging nature and character will be precious to my children. May there be comfort in knowing that You, the timeless and eternal One, know them, hold them, have plans for them, and, most of all, love them.

Amen.

Casting all your care on Him,
because He cares about you. — 1 Peter 5:7

Bearer of our Burdens,

I want my children to develop a strong prayer life—
not a once or twice daily appointed time to talk with you
but a steady, ongoing, unending conversation throughout
the day.

Having this trait will help them bring any and every
immediate concern right to Your throne room. May my
children be so confident in Your care and concern for
them that they tell You anything that causes questions
or pain. May they give over to You all their discontent,
discouragement, and despair.

May my children not struggle with worry because
they choose to hand their cares to You and trust in Your
sufficiency for all they face.

Amen.

For the LORD has comforted His people, and will
have compassion on His afflicted ones. — Isaiah 49:13

God of all Comfort,

During times of stress, trial, and sadness throughout
my children's lives, I pray that they will know Your Holy
Spirit as their Comforter. May Your Spirit bring to my
children's minds verses from Your Word about Your
sovereignty, Your wisdom, Your power, and how You
work in all things for their good. May Your Word help
give them the right perspective.

Will You allow them to know Your nearness in
everything they face? Thank You that my children can
know You as Immanuel—God with us. May this give
them strength and courage.

Thank You that even in those difficult times when I
can't be there with my children, You will be with them as
their Comforter.

Amen.

I have given you the authority to trample on snakes and scorpions and over all the power of the enemy. — Luke 10:19

Powerful Conqueror of Hell and the Grave,

Because we are "in You," we can be triumphant over the powers of evil. We need not fear Satan and his demons, for their doom is sure.

I know that at points along the way, the enemy will come against my children—maybe through some plan to cause them to stumble, maybe to help establish some unholy and unhealthy habit or some other dark and sinister way.

May my children resist the attack and fearlessly stand strong, trusting and obeying You. May the enemy's ploys be crushed and no stronghold be allowed to form in my children's lives.

Amen.

The LORD is my light and my salvation—whom shall
I fear? The LORD is the stronghold of my life—
of whom shall I be afraid? – Psalm 27:1

Our Strength,

Fear like a dark shadow may sometimes fall across
my children's hearts. It may be because they enter into
an unknown situation, facing someone who makes them
anxious or encountering danger.

I ask, Lord, that in each of those times may Your
Word and Your promises come back to the mind of my
children. May they recall verses that strengthen them as
they consider Your sovereignty, Your power, and Your
presence. May the holy light of Your Word push back the
shadows from their heart and mind.

Because of their faith, may they find themselves
ready to boldly face whatever is before them.

Amen.

Therefore, everyone who hears these words
of Mine and acts on them will be like a sensible man
who built his house on the rock. — Matthew 7:24

Master,

Even if my children are rich in opportunities to hear
Your Word, if they do not act upon it, it is of no benefit to
them. I pray that my children will be doers of Your Word.
May they be wise and love Your instruction.

As they hear Your Word, may they search their own
heart to see what the application should be. May they be
tenderhearted and willing to make whatever changes are
required in their habits and lifestyle. May they be quick to
carry out whatever You are instructing them to do.

When the difficult storms of life come, may my
children endure, faith strong and intact because they trust
in You and You alone.

Amen.

There came a voice from heaven: This is My beloved Son.
I take delight in Him! — Matthew 3:17

Our Encourager,

So often I will speak words of love and affection to
my children. I pray today Lord that through Your Holy
Spirit's work, not just my children's ears but their hearts
also may hear these words.

May they have an unshakable confidence in how
loved and wanted they are. May they always feel my
acceptance of them.

It's not coincidental that Your words in today's
passage were spoken before Jesus had actually "done"
anything—before the miracles, before the teaching. May
my children deeply hear me say that apart from any and all
achievements, I love them fully and simply for who they
are. Please allow this truth to take root in their soul and
give them great confidence and may it bear much fruit for
Your glory.

Amen.

Surely You desire integrity
in the inner self. — Psalm 51:6

The One Who Is Truth,

It's not a matter of *if* but *when* children will lie. Like all fallen people, at times they will be tempted to avoid the truth, and at some points they will give into that temptation. May the training in our home imprint on my children what a detestable thing lying is in the eyes of God.

May my children choose early that the path of honesty is wisest for them and the one that they always wish to follow. May they never get away with even a small lie. Please always quickly lead them to confession.

Would You guide them to so value truthfulness that they will not tolerate even small lies from their closest friends?

Amen.

Then He said to His disciples, "The harvest is abundant but the workers are few. Therefore, pray to the Lord of the harvest to send out workers into His harvest."
— Matthew 9:37–38

Lord of the Harvest,

I pray that my children will have opportunities to hear a number of missionaries speak of their work. May this make a great and lasting impression on their heart. As my children grow, may they also read stories of great mission workers.

If You would so bless and allow, may my children have an opportunity to participate in short-term mission trips—local, regional, and, if possible, even international. May these greatly mark their heart with love for all people and a desire for all to know Your good news.

Would You give my children a spirit that sees their school, sport's teams, and circle of friends as potential mission fields?

Amen.

LORD, who is like You among the gods?
Who is like You, glorious in holiness, revered
with praises, performing wonders? — Exodus 15:11

Almighty King of Heaven,

I come today desiring that my children will know You for who You truly are and will respond with reverence. May they have a deep certainty that there is none like You in heaven or on earth. You alone are God.

May their words of praise flow from the love and wonder in their hearts. May they live with a holy awe for You. May their daily actions and words to others also be acts of worship as they serve You with all they are.

May their great desire be to see You exalted and worshipped for who You are.

Amen.

I will praise You because I have been remarkably
and wonderfully made. Your works are wonderful,
and I know this very well. – Psalm 139:14

Creator,

I come today asking that at some point along the way
may my children not just believe the passage above, but
may they also feel it. May they fully embrace that they are
divinely designed by You. May they trust that You have
made countless choices of details about them—their body
type, hair texture, eye color, complexion, fingerprints.
May they trust that You have skillfully created them and
that You are pleased with how You have made them.

May this be a strength and a confidence in their life,
but may it never lead to pride or arrogance in any way.
Please guide them to maintain a healthy balance at this
point. May they rightly see themselves as You do.

May their confidence in Your good works and in
Your acceptance of them be a fortress that keeps them
strong when facing esteem issues that plague so many
teens and young adults.

Amen.

He has rescued us from the dominion of darkness and
transferred us into the kingdom of the Son He loves.
– Colossians 1:13

Redeemer,

Some people have radical and dramatic stories of
coming to You in faith. Others may have grown up in a
Christian home, been around people of faith their entire
life, and then one day gently embrace You as their own
Savior and Lord. However it happens, all praise and honor
goes to You!

One day my children may be called on to tell of their
personal experience of accepting You as their Lord and
Savior. Regardless of the earthly details of the story, may
they be certain of the spiritual reality that at one point
they were a part of the kingdom of darkness, and then
they were rescued, redeemed, and brought into Your
everlasting kingdom of light.

Will You use my children's stories for Your glory?

Amen.

A man who finds a wife finds a good thing and obtains favor from the LORD. – Proverbs 18:22

Cornerstone,

Perhaps Your plan for my children includes their remaining single, but if it doesn't, I pray that You would help them find the right partner at the right time. May they know a clear leading from You regarding this relationship, and would You guide them to make a choice not merely on physical attraction but on true love, commitment, and an ability for two people to serve You together better than they could alone.

Through their relationship together, may they truly know the grace of life that is found in an intimate union that You have blessed. May they always have You as the center of their relationship and as the foundation that they build a life upon together.

Will You guard them from divorce? May there never even be a hint of infidelity, and will You guard them from that temptation? May there never be any abuse but rather a beautiful unity that for decades reflects the evidence that You dwell closely with them.

Prepare both of them even today for what You have for them together in the future.

Amen.

Peace I leave with you. My peace I give to you.
I do not give to you as the world gives. — John 14:27

Prince of Peace,

This fallen world has always been a place of unrest and turmoil. It will only intensify as we come closer to Your return. Your prophecies are full of unsettling events yet to occur as time runs down for this world.

I pray that my children will know peace in their hearts that cannot be unseated by any circumstance or event. May they have that constant abiding peace that comes only from knowing You. May they have a deep and eternally settled sense that "all is well" between them and their Maker. May this calm weather any situations that try to shake it.

May my children have a peaceful spirit and sleep well at night because of faith and confidence in You.

Amen.

Rebellion is like the sin of divination, and defiance
is like wickedness and idolatry. — 1 Samuel 15:23

Most High God,

Many believe that teen rebellion is just a normal phase all kids go through. I do not. I believe all children will test the limits to see if the consequences will indeed be as they were instructed they would be. A wise child will learn and submit. A foolish child will persist in doing wrong.

Any rebellion is simply pride fully expressed. It is the immature cry of "I want what I want when I want it." Its twin sister, stubbornness, will cause a child to become arrogant, defiant, and stuck in their place of pride.

God, please guide me with wisdom to identify early the moments of pride, selfishness, and stubbornness in my child's life. May You and I together lead my child to have a humble, submissive heart—one that is in a position to be richly blessed by You.

Amen.

In the day of prosperity be joyful, but in the day of adversity,
consider: God has made the one as well as the other.
— Ecclesiastes 7:14

Lord of All,

Life is filled with such uncertainty. We all have a mix
of good days and hard days. There is no way any of us can
really predict what lies around the bend for us. The future
is in Your hand, and You are sovereign over it all.

I pray that both kinds of days will cause my children
to consider the Giver of the day. In the good times may
they always be mindful to express their gratitude to You
for even the simple joys.

In the hard times may Your sovereignty be a
comfort to them. May they trust that You have allowed
the difficulties for a perfect reason. May they know Your
nearness in these times, and even as they endure, may they
be at peace.

Amen.

From eternity to eternity,
You are God. — Psalm 90:2

Eternal King,

You exist outside of time. You are without beginning.
You are without end. You have always been and will always
be. In this very moment You exist perfectly in the past, in
the present, as well as in the future. You are never younger
and never older—truly timeless.

I pray that as my children consider this unfathomable
truth about You, may it lead them to awe and wonder.
Would You have them to be aware of how brief this
mortal life really is and how precious is every moment and
opportunity we have?

Would You guide them to worship You for the
privilege of being with You forever?

Amen.

Instruct a wise man, and he will be wiser still;
teach a righteous man, and he will learn more.
— Proverbs 9:9

Source of All Wisdom,

All truth comes from You. The longing for truth is in the fabric of our souls. Only You can truly satisfy our desire for wisdom.

I pray that my children will have teachable spirits, particularly when it comes to Your Word. May they want to know You ever deeper.

I pray also regarding the variety of classroom teachers that they will have as they grow. May my children be the kind of students that are a joy for a teacher because of their desire to learn. As instruction and correction come their way, may they welcome it so as to grow and be prepared for what You have ahead for them.

Amen.

Teach us to number our days carefully so that we may
develop wisdom in our hearts. — Psalm 90:12

Timeless One,

My children cannot yet appreciate, as I do, the brevity
of life. But they will learn as they grow that our days truly
are a brief morning mist that is here and then gone.

I pray that my children will believe that every day
they live is a gift from You and that as the Giver of each
day You know how it can best be spent. May they seek You
for how they can wisely use the precious time they have on
this planet.

May they live their days for Your glory, seeing each as
a gift they can give back to You.

Amen.

The fruit of the Spirit
is . . . self-control. — Galatians 5:22

All-Powerful Yet Tender King,

Because You are perfect in all actions and expressions, there is never a need for You to show restraint. Yet, because we are fallen, we need Your Spirit to produce within us self-control.

I pray that my children will learn to model this with excellence. For Your glory may they show restraint in their passions and appetites. May they not vent every emotion and thought they think and feel.

May their behavior reflect a wisdom that comes from the presence of your Holy Spirit.

Amen.

How can a young man keep his way pure?
By keeping Your word. — Psalm 119:9

Wonderful Counselor,

Some people seem bent on making every mistake themselves, and they learn lessons that way. Others, the wise ones, look to other people to guide them away from danger and into blessing.

I pray that my children will be among the wise ones who know from a young age that there is no better way to live a life than to seek Your wisdom for all of their steps. May they make time daily to be in Your Word. May they never approach Your book out of duty but out of desire.

May their life be an endless upward spiral of "the more they trust You, the more blessed their life is" and "the more blessed their life is, the more they want to trust You."

Amen.

Set your minds on what is above,
not on what is on the earth. — Colossians 3:2

The Way to Life,

Throughout the day so many things will scream for
my children's attention. Many of these things will be petty
and insignificant. I pray that in the midst of it all, my
children's minds will be like a compass pointing to true
north, the kingdom of heaven.

I pray that their focus and attention throughout all
their days will be on the principles and realities of things
above. Though they walk through a world of things that
are temporal, may their eyes and thoughts be on the
eternal. May this change everything about their priorities.

Amen.

Teach a youth about the way he should go;
even when he is old he will not depart from it.
– Proverbs 22:6

Loving Father,

Some things in life I have done Your way. When I did, I was always glad. Some things in life I have done my own way. I have always been regretful when this occurred. The responsibility of raising a child is one that I definitely want to fully do Your way.

Help me train my children early according to Your wisdom so they might develop lifelong habits that will bring blessing. Will You be gracious to me and guide me to recall appropriate Scripture verses to use in teachable moments with my children? Please help me seek out and find great godly wisdom for this task and not be led by ever-changing worldly thinking.

Will You help me guide them in ways that are best for their unique design?

Amen.

Whatever you do, do it enthusiastically, as something done
for the Lord and not for men. — Colossians 3:23

Most Excellent One,

I pray that my children will value excellence in all
they do. May they trust that whatever the task before
them—work around the house, school assignments,
projects at their job—it is one You have allowed to come
their way, and may they desire to reflect Your character in
how they work.

May their diligence be a great source of blessing to
them.

Will You please guide them to pursue this in a
healthy, holy way and not in a legalistic, compulsive,
unhealthy, unbalanced manner?

Amen.

The one who conceals his sins will not prosper, but whoever
confesses and renounces them will find mercy.
– Proverbs 28:13

Our Forgiver,

Sometimes when my children are not in my presence,
they will face temptation. Because You are a Redeemer,
You can even use the times when they fail to help them
learn strategies for how to stand strong the next time they
face the same sin.

Sometimes when my children sin in some way, no
one besides You and them knows about it. I pray in those
moments that because of Your Spirit's prompting, my
children will be quick to confess and seek forgiveness. May
they not continue to conceal their failure. May their heart
be tender and obedient to Your earliest call to confession.

May the sweetness of the mercy and grace they will
surely find with You lead them to continue to be prompt
in confessing their sin.

Amen.

I will seek refuge in the shadow of
Your wings until danger passes. — Psalm 57:1

Our Refuge,

We see a picture of You as a caring parent in today's verse. What a comfort it is that this is Your heart for Your children.

There will be times when I can't be there to provide shelter and protection for my children. I pray they will learn early the wisdom of calling out to You in these moments. May they run to You and find that You are a faithful refuge for them. May they find that You physically protect them, and may their spirit find that when they move near to Your side, there is always calm and peace.

Amen.

"Follow Me," He told them, "and I will make
you fish for people!" – Matthew 4:19

Savior,

I pray often that my children will be so captured and
consumed by Your beautiful gospel that it is ever on their
minds. May they live with an awe and wonder that in Your
great mercy You have redeemed them.

May this amazement lead them to want others
to know the gift of salvation You offer. May it be their
heartbeat to see others rescued from the kingdom of
darkness and brought into Your kingdom of light.

May they speak boldly and unashamedly that they
believe You are the way, the truth, and the life and that no
one comes to the Father except through You. Would You
lead them to know the incredible blessing of seeing those
with whom they share the gospel come to faith?

Amen.

Deliver me, my God, from the power of the wicked,
from the grasp of the unjust and oppressive. – Psalm 71:4

Our Defender,

At some point, hopefully later than sooner, my children will have to deal with peers who will try to intimidate and take advantage of them. I pray even now that You will prepare my children for that moment.

May they be secure in knowing Your hand is on their life and that You can take care of them and lead them through the situation. May they be able to look beyond the immediate tension and emotion of the moment and consider the heart and soul of the one oppressing them.

May they cry out to You in that time for Your deliverance. Will Your Spirit's nearness calm their fear, give them words of wisdom, and protect them?

May they even pray for the salvation of the one offending them. If You allow them opportunity, may my children express their forgiveness to them.

Amen.

Praising and cursing come out of the same mouth.
My brothers, these things should not be this way.
Does a spring pour out sweet and bitter water
from the same opening? Can a fig tree produce olives,
my brothers, or a grapevine produce figs? Neither can a
saltwater spring yield fresh water. — James 3:10–12

Lover of Purity,

I pray that as my children grow, especially as teenagers
and into young adulthood, there will be consistency in
their language at all times. May they not speak one way at
home and another lesser and looser way with their friends.

May the punch and power of profanity never hold
an attraction for them or the friends they choose to be
around. May the words they bring to You in worship and
devotion be consistent with how they speak in all times
of their life.

Amen.

According to the grace given to us,
we have different gifts. – Romans 12:6

Creator,

Not only have You amazingly created us physically; You have formed each of us with unique combinations of spiritual gifts. The varieties and combinations of gifting are mind-blowing, and You have formed each of us with great purpose as to how we can serve You. As we serve You with our gifting, it will mean glory for You and joy for us.

I can't imagine yet all You have placed within my children, but I live with great anticipation for their gifting to be revealed in time. All types of gifting are exciting—wisdom, knowledge, faith, serving, encouraging, giving, mercy, helping with needs of others, and leadership.

I don't have specific dreams for what I would like my children's vocations and/or ministry to look like; I simply want them to seek after Your leading and to discover what You have specifically wired them for. Will You guide them on the journey of discovering their gifts and their places of service?

Amen.

Don't get drunk with wine, which leads to reckless actions,
but be filled by the Spirit. – Ephesians 5:18

Lord,

The best of life is always found when all we are is
submitted to Your control. When Your Holy Spirit fills
and directs a believer, the outcome will always ultimately
be joy, peace, hope, and untold good things.

I pray that my children will not give over control of
themselves, even for brief periods of time, to anything
or anyone other than You. They may be tempted with a
number of substances, legal and illegal, along the way; but
may they see the value and holy wisdom in not allowing
themselves to be mastered by anything other than You.

Please guide them with the strength to stand strong
and resist temptation. May they choose instead to hold to
the freedom You give.

Amen.

Therefore, as we have opportunity, we must work
for the good of all, especially for those who belong
to the household of faith. — Galatians 6:10

Good Shepherd,

In a world where people are so used to seeing others behave in ways that are unkind and self-serving, You have called us to be a different and peculiar people. It will seem strange and fascinating to the world to watch people who actively seek opportunities to do good to others.

I pray that my children will be among those people the world will see always speaking and showing kindness and love to others.

May this simply be the fruitful overflow of Your love within them.

Amen.

Be diligent to present yourself approved to God,
a worker who doesn't need to be ashamed,
correctly teaching the word of truth. — 2 Timothy 2:15

Most Excellent God,

I ask today that You would put within my children's hearts the desire to pursue excellence in all their endeavors. May they never be accused of being lazy, and may they wisely choose the things to which they will give their efforts and energy.

Would You guide them to be self-motivated and driven in a healthy way? May this determination show in their schoolwork, in their jobs and employment. May they be zealous about doing quality work.

May this come from their desire to reflect Your excellence in all things.

Amen.

How happy is the man who does not follow
the advice of the wicked or take the path of sinners
or join a group of mockers. – Psalm 1:1

Deliverer,

As my children's world expands, there will more and
more acquaintances that as a parent I might consider "bad
influences." Some of these will be what Your Word would
call fools. I ask in those moments of first encounter that
Your Spirit would be active in my children's hearts.

The wisest thing for them would be simply not to let
themselves be engaged by the unwise. May they certainly
not linger in these relationships.

May they know Your Spirit's leading, and may they
heed Your voice telling them to simply walk away.

Amen.

To the pure, everything is pure, but to those who are defiled and unbelieving nothing is pure; in fact, both their mind and conscience are defiled. — Titus 1:15

Holy King of Heaven,

I pray today asking that my children will be pure minded. May they retain a childlikeness and innocence about them.

There will be times when they hear punch lines, sexual references, and innuendos and not comprehend the meaning. May they have peace in those moments knowing that to pursue the meaning would simply lead them down shadowed hallways and into darker places. May they be content simply to let it pass them by.

May they be pure in heart, always believing for the best in others and seeking for Your honor in all situations. Will You continue to refine them that all sin and worldly affections may be confessed? May the focus of their heart and mind be singularly set on Your glory.

Amen.

For we brought nothing into the world, and we
can take nothing out. But if we have food and clothing,
we will be content with these. — 1 Timothy 6:7–8

Satisfier of our Souls,

I know at some point along the way, the clawing
fingers of money, consumerism, and possessions will strive
to place their grip around my children's hearts. I pray this
will always only be a temporary state that is quickly ended.
May my children have great faith in You as the Provider
of their daily bread and clothing. May they choose to
value and pursue treasures that are eternal and not the
temporary ones that moths and rust destroy.

May my children find their riches in their relationship
to You and in relationships with others. May they know
clearly how to discern between their wants and their
needs, and may they choose wisely and accordingly.

Amen.

Before his downfall a man's heart is proud,
but humility comes before honor. — Proverbs 18:12

Excellent One,

I pray that my children will have right perspective. May they always see You as being first and foremost in importance. May they also be mindful to consider others as more important than themselves.

Would You guard them from slipping into the shadow lands of pride? Would You guide them to be so content with Your sufficiency and Your love for them that they don't feel the need to exalt themselves? Would You help them be aware of pride when they see it expressed in others and to be so turned off by it that they want to make sure never to let it take root in their own heart?

May there be many times when because of the humble, quiet, excellent way my children go about their work, others recognize them and honor them for what they do.

Amen.

If we confess our sins, He is faithful and righteous to forgive us our sins and to cleanse us from all unrighteousness.
– 1 John 1:9

Faithful Forgiver,

I don't live under any illusion that my children will live the lives of perfect saints. I do know that they will make mistakes, have failures, and even have moments of rebellion against what is right. I ask that these moments will not be the pattern of their lives, and may the episodes be few and far between.

When my children sin, Lord, I pray they will be fast in asking for forgiveness. May they be tender and sensitive to Your Spirit's voice of conviction.

In their moments of confession, I ask that today's passage would be a jewel they treasure and return to often. May it give them confidence and peace because of the certainty of Your grace and cleansing.

Amen.

If anyone competes as an athlete, he is not crowned unless
he competes according to the rules. — 2 Timothy 2:5

Righteous Judge,

I do pray that my children will have a fiery
competitive streak. However, may they allow this part of
their personality to be under Your lordship, and may it
show itself in ways which are good and holy.

I do pray that in sporting activities, their school
studies, and in artistic ventures my children will strive to be
excellent and victorious. May they model determination
and perseverance. May they also be committed to fairness.

I pray that in their spiritual life they will strive with
zeal and great discipline to be victorious over their own
flesh and selfish desires. May they pursue the prize of
knowing and experiencing You more.

Amen.

How I love Your instruction!
It is my meditation all day long. – Psalm 119:97

Heavenly Father,

I pray that I teach my children to love Your Word deeply through example and not just instruction. I know that they will observe so many moments in my life when I don't think they are looking. May they catch me going to Your Word on so many occasions in life.

May they see in me a reverence, desire, and love for Scripture. May they see it bear fruit in my life such that they desire it for their own life.

May it be that my words of teaching for why they should love Your Word will be few because they just "get it" through the example that is set.

Bless You for Your perfect, holy Word. May it shine brightly from my life onto my children.

Amen.

How happy is everyone who fears the LORD, who walks in His ways! Your wife will be like a fruitful vine within your house; your sons, like young olive trees around your table.
– Psalm 128: 1, 3

Great Provider,

Our meals together have been and will always be sweet times of family togetherness. It is so important to take time out of a busy day to sit together and remember Your provisions. I am thankful for the opportunity to hear about everyone's day. Often in times like these, I will be given a window into the hearts of my children.

I pray that You grant me wisdom to read the moments well as we eat and talk. Help me know when to properly instruct, comfort, encourage, dream . . . whatever is needed in the moment. I invite You to dwell closely with us in these times, and may You be honored through our love, conversation, and laughter together.

Amen.

Everyone must submit to the governing authorities,
for there is no authority except from God, and those
that exist are instituted by God. – Romans 13:1

God of Order,

You have established the pattern of authority and
submission throughout all things. We see it within the
Trinity. We see it in the church. We see it in families. We
see it in work relations.

I pray that my children will take You at Your
Word, trust You, and will willingly submit to all levels of
leadership, if that leadership is in alignment with Your
Word. I pray that in their classrooms, on athletic teams,
and in places of employment, may my children be among
those who willingly submit to leadership and cannot be
swayed into rebellion.

Amen.

Love the Lord your God with all your heart, with all your
soul, with all your mind, and with all your strength.
– Mark 12:30

Our Loving Father,

You know how passionately and persistently I pray
that my children will have a right relationship with You.
Of all the words that might describe their relationship
with You, may the one that looms the largest be: LOVE.

May they, as You call them to in Your Word, love
You with every part of who they are—with all their being,
with all their emotion and passion, with all their thoughts
and intellect, as well as with all their physical capabilities.
May their love never be empty words or empty ritual but
instead always be living and active.

Please guide their life to give evidence that this is a
priority to them.

Amen.

The fruit of the Spirit is . . . joy. — Galatians 5:22

Giver of Joy,

To know You, Lord, is to know joy. I pray that through all of their life, my children will know that deep-down sense of well-being that comes when all is right between someone and their Maker.

May this overflow of knowing You produce real hope and peace. May it remain strong and unaffected by circumstances or anything anyone else might do or say to them.

You were able to endure the worst of earthly moments for the joy of the relationship You had with the Father. May my children endure the hard times they face and never lose the joy of simply belonging to You.

Amen.

Rejoice with those who rejoice; weep
with those who weep. – Romans 12:15

Perfect One,

You have so graciously filled Your people with Your
Spirit so that we have power to act in situations in ways
that are not the norm and are actually supernatural. In our
flesh we may be resentful of the successes of others and
delight in their hardships. Because of Your Spirit, we can
move toward them and join with them in what they are
experiencing in life.

I pray that my children will be so trusting of Your
good hand in their lives that they are actually free to share
joy with others who are experiencing blessings and honor.

May my children also be moved to show kindness
and compassion toward others in difficult situations.
Would You help them in love to shed tears with others
facing times of disappointment, hardship, or sorrow?

Amen.

Don't you know that your body is a sanctuary
of the Holy Spirit. — 1 Corinthians 6:19

Creator,

I pray that my children will be mindful of being stewards of the physical body You have given them. Because their body, along with all they have, belongs to You, it is Yours to use. May my children be excellent in the care and stewardship of it.

May they have the strength to fight bad impulses in making food choices. May they stay away from, or at least use good discretion and moderation in making decisions about, snack food. When given the opportunity, may they stay away from alcohol, tobacco products, and drugs.

I pray that my children will adopt a healthy lifestyle— good nutrition, exercise, getting adequate sleep. May they present their body to You as a living sacrifice for Your glory.

Amen.

Do not grumble. – I Corinthians 10:10 NIV

God of All Provision,

Throughout history You have had a people who tasted richly of Your physical and spiritual provision and yet became self-centered and grumbling. I ask that this would not ever be true of my children.

Would You guide them to trust in Your love, Your will, and Your provision for them that even during the leaner seasons of life, they will not complain? Would You guide them to trust that You have chosen the ones who are to be in positions of authority over them and may they willingly, even joyfully, submit?

Would You weed out any self-centeredness within their heart that their speech will never be that of discontentment toward You? Please guide them to have a contented, peaceful, patient, and trusting heart.

Amen.

He does what He wants with the army of heaven
and the inhabitants of the earth. – Daniel 4:35

Most High God,

You are sovereign. You reign from the throne of
heaven. You do throughout all creation what pleases You,
and whatever You do, You do with perfection. There is
no throne higher than Yours; no power in heaven, hell, or
on earth can thwart Your plans. All people, creatures, and
objects do Your bidding.

As my children come to learn this truth about You, I
pray it will bring them enduring comfort. May they trust
that You are in charge of their life and that anything that
comes against them (trials, afflictions, problems) has
already passed through Your hand and You are allowing
it for a good reason. May it give them peace that not one
moment of their life is without a plan and purpose.

May they find great rest in Your sovereignty.

Amen.

Whoever is faithful in very little is also faithful
in much, and whoever is unrighteous in very little
is also unrighteous in much. — Luke 16:10

Master,

Bless You that You love us enough to deal with each of us individually. You give us all unique and differing talents and responsibilities and hold us accountable for what we do with them.

I pray that as my children are given new responsibilities from You, may they never resent a task they feel is beneath their abilities. May they instead trust that You are working perfectly, and therefore the wisest choice for them is to be excellent in the work before them. May my children prove their faithfulness by being responsible for the little that is theirs to do.

May this hold true not just in how they handle talents but in how they handle their finances as well. Would You bless their faithfulness with a greater capacity for service here on earth as well as one day in Your kingdom?

Amen.

But as for me, God's presence is my good. – Psalm 73:28

The One Who Loves Us,

I pray today that my children will always have a desire to draw near to You. May they find that even from a young age, when time is spent in Your presence, life makes sense, perspective is gained, and days go well.

May my children greatly desire times of corporate gathering to worship You. Please help them come to love time alone in Your Word, hearing Your heart and sitting at Your feet.

May their longing for intimacy with You be a flame in their soul that simply grows stronger through each passing year of their life.

Amen.

Flee from idolatry. — 1 Corinthians 10:14

One True God,

We are a people who have been made to worship. There are longings deep within us—desires for love, beauty, purpose, significance, acceptance—that are meant to lead us to You. These desires are only truly satisfied when we have our whole focus fixed on You.

Yet many will look to other things to satisfy these longings. While I don't really fear that my children will bow down to a figure of wood or stone, other idols will strive to get a grip on their hearts.

God, will You guard and protect them from ever trying to find deep meaning and satisfaction from the idols of this world such as power, popularity, status, achievement, success, money, appearance, and approval? These are all insidious vines that begin to get a grip on our heart. May my children have success in rejecting them as a source of true meaning and hope.

May they continually choose to love only You as the one who is on the throne of their life.

Amen.

For You are my rock and my fortress;
You lead and guide me because of Your name. — Psalm 31:3

God Who Leads,

I pray that my children will know the adventure of faith—that place where Your calling is clear, the task is great, and their own power and wisdom are not sufficient for the work. If it is going to be done, You're going to have to accomplish it. Yet You invite them to join You in achieving great things.

Though they may feel overwhelmed by the challenges before them, may they trust You. May they not play it safe. May they risk. May they go beyond their comfort zone and step out, deeply aware of their constant need of and dependence on You.

As a result, may they know You and Your faithfulness as they would never know You otherwise.

Amen.

You are the salt of the earth. . . .
You are the light of the world. – Matthew 5:13–14

Savior,

Because we've been forever changed by Your grace, we will stand out as being different from the people of this world. I pray that just as salt in biblical times was used primarily as a preservative, my children's righteousness will help slow the decay of this present world. I pray that their lives will be a seasoning that leads people of the world to thirst for the hope my children have found in You.

I pray also that their life will shine as a godly example of Your great power. May their words and actions testify of Your grace and mercy. May they never be afraid or ashamed to be known as Yours, but with boldness may their good deeds burn bright before a watching world.

Amen.

Why do you look at the speck in your brother's eye
but don't notice the log in your own eye? — Matthew 7:3

Perfect Judge,

I pray that You would guard my children from ever having a critical spirit. May they never develop a spirit of pride where they look at others and feel self-satisfied or superior. May they never feel that it is their place to pass judgment on others.

May they instead be so aware of their own shortcomings and the goodness of the grace that has been extended to them that they maintain a gentle, humble spirit.

May they indeed try to help others who have failures in their life; yet may they do it from a place of love and tender caring.

Amen.

Make every effort to keep the unity of the Spirit
through the bond of peace. – Ephesians 4:3 NIV

One Who Speaks Peace,

In a world where the natural thing to do is to be selfish and demand one's way, that choice will always result in tension and a lack of unity. I pray that my children will instead pursue the pattern of Your kingdom.

Would You guide my children to seek to maintain peace in relationships? May they have a gentle humility that gives them great patience in dealing with others. Would You guide them not to be easily angered and always quick to forgive?

Amen.

Don't love sleep, or you will become poor; open your eyes,
and you'll have enough to eat. – Proverbs 20:13

Our Fervent God,

You have given us work to do that will give our lives
meaning. By being diligent and excellent, we can reflect
Your character to the world and bring You glory.

I pray that my children will never be lazy but will
be intentional and excellent in whatever work is before
them. May they please You with an industrious spirit and
good work ethic. May they bring joy to those who have
given them assignments to do.

May my children always be blessed with the good
reward that comes to those who work hard and provide
well for members of their families. May they never know
the lack of respect that comes to those who are lazy and
unmotivated.

Amen.

Your beauty should not consist of outward things like elaborate hairstyles and the wearing of gold ornaments or fine clothes. Instead, it should consist of what is inside the heart with the imperishable quality of a gentle and quiet spirit, which is very valuable in God's eyes. — 1 Peter 3:3–4

Creator,

Even from a young age, my children will encounter thousands of messages trying to tell them what "beautiful" is as it relates to women. As they struggle to put together what their definition of beauty is, I pray that my children will wholeheartedly trust the truth of Your Word speaking to them.

This will be against the grain of the culture, but will You lead them to value the beauty of a woman's quiet, gentle spirit far above any look that can be gained through makeup and temporary fashion trends? May they believe that spiritual virtue always is more important than external appearance.

May my children value what is imperishable over what is temporary and fading.

Amen.

For the love of money is a root of all kinds of evil, and by craving it, some have wandered away from the faith and pierced themselves with many pains. – 1 Timothy 6:10

God Who Is Our Inheritance,

I want my children to always pursue higher things. I want their hearts to be set on the kingdom above and not on the temporary kingdom of now.

May they realize that they are simply a steward of all that You entrust them with. If You choose them to steward a great amount of earthly riches, that's wonderful, but may they never have a love for money.

May they always wisely discern the difference between their wants and their needs. May they live like all of their wealth, not just a portion, belongs to You.

Amen.

If you have faith the size of a mustard seed, you will tell this mountain, "Move from here to there," and it will move. Nothing will be impossible for you. — Matthew 17:20

The One Who Is Worthy of Our Faith,

I ask that the measure of faith that You gift my children with will always be an active, growing, maturing faith. As new circumstances and situations come along, I pray they will trust You as You lead them. May they have full confidence that "things not seen" are just as real as the things their eyes can see.

I pray that they will be so sure of Your existence, Your holiness, Your glory, Your love, and Your nearness that it is a guiding principal for all of their decisions. May they have courage to take chances and brave steps of faith to follow Your lead. May it give them great strength trusting that if any venture, plan, or dream is in accordance with Your will, then nothing is impossible.

Amen.

I have treasured Your word in my heart so that
I may not sin against You. — Psalm 119:11

Word of God,

I come today asking that You might give my children the gift of memorizing Your Word. If You should not make it easy, would You let them see the benefit of it and have a desire to do the hard work anyway?

I pray that they will commit verses and passages to memory that will help them recognize the early approach of the enemy. May these verses also direct them on how to live a holy life that is easy for You to bless.

It's not enough for them simply to know Your Word and recognize sin, but may they apply Your truth to every area and relationship of their life and be a doer of Your Word.

Amen.

Now we ask you, brothers, to give recognition
to those who labor among you and lead you in the Lord
and admonish you, and to regard them very highly in love
because of their work. — 1 Thessalonians 5:12–13

Great Shepherd,

Today I come to lift up our pastor and other ministers to You—and particularly their relationship with my children. May they truly be leaders of great integrity who are intimately hearing You speak truth into their lives. May they passionately love and obey You.

From that overflow may their ministry be significant to my children. From the pulpit may they help ground my children in the truth of Your Word. In personal interaction may their care and concern be meaningful to my children.

While I pray for our pastor, I also want to be mindful of other teachers and leaders at our church. May my children's time with them be fruitful and used by You for growth. May our family always have an attitude of respect, appreciation, and honor for our spiritual leaders.

Amen.

Whatever your hands find to do,
do with all your strength. — Ecclesiastes 9:10

Master,

At some point in life, my children will find themselves caught in a transitional or waiting season. Maybe they aren't in a class or school program that they wish to be in, or maybe it's not quite the job they were hoping for. Whenever this happens, may they still pursue excellence in what they do.

Would You help them maintain hope trusting that You fully see where they are and where You have allowed them to be in the time of waiting? May they commit themselves to doing the best they can with what is before them at every moment. Though it may be work they feel is not a good fit for them, or may even be beneath their abilities, may they take it on with a passion for excellence.

Amen.

For I am persuaded that not even death or life, angels or
rulers, things present or things to come, hostile powers,
height or depth, or any other created thing will have the
power to separate us from the love of God that is
in Christ Jesus our Lord. — Romans 8:38–39

Unchanging One,

I come before You today asking that my children will
not wrestle with doubts about whether or not You love
them. May they always see Your cross as the final word
declaring just how totally, fully, and eternally they are
loved.

May they find today's verse to be one of great comfort
and assurance to them. Though they may face hardship,
trouble, danger, temptation, persecution, and even death
for You, may they never wonder if they are securely held in
Your love. Though their love for You may at times falter,
may they live never questioning whether anything can
separate them from Your great love.

Amen.

My bones were not hidden from You when I was
made in secret, when I was formed in the depths of the
earth. Your eyes saw me when I was formless;
all my days were written in Your book and planned
before a single one of them began. – Psalm 139:15–16

One and Only God,

You have formed no one else in all of history who is
exactly like my children. Bless You God of inexhaustible
creativity!

In a world where there is such pressure to conform
to whatever is current, would You have my children to
be at peace with being who they uniquely are? May this
be a strength that allows them to pursue their individual
passions and dreams. May they be victorious over the
temptations to compare themselves to others.

Would You help my children have courage to pursue
the path in life You uniquely offer to them? May they find
it a joy and an adventure to be an original.

Amen.

Pray at all times in the Spirit with every prayer
and request. – Ephesians 6:18

God Who Hears Our Hearts,

My children will often hear my voice praying—
blessings for meals, lifting up concerns for our family,
intercession for friends.

In the midst of all those prayers, Lord, please make
me mindful to let my children hear my heart. May I be
mindful at times to give voice to prayers that focus on me.

May I speak my trust in You. May I make known my
words of praise and adoration of You. Please guide me to
speak aloud my words of confession and repentance.

May my children not just hear "words" but actually
witness my heart coming before Your throne.

Amen.

Please test your servants for 10 days. Let us be given
vegetables to eat and water to drink. Then examine
our appearance and the appearance of the young men
who are eating the king's food. — Daniel 1:12–13

Way of Life,

I know that my children, like everyone, will be
attracted to brightly packaged, highly advertised, and
nutritionally void foods. I pray that they will walk with
great wisdom in making choices related to food and
beverage.

Would You give them an attraction to good, healthy
meats and grains, vegetables and fruits, and water as a
beverage of choice? Would You guide them to enjoy
making good decisions as well as enjoying the results of
those wise choices?

I know they will be tempted by lesser choices, but
would You lead them to live with great self-control and
moderation. Would You help them not develop poor
habits, and please keep them from any struggles with
eating disorders?

May they enjoy blessing You for the excellent foods
You provide for us.

Amen.

The Lord is very compassionate
and merciful. — James 5:11

Our Tenderhearted Savior,

You were moved with mercy by our fallen condition,
and You took action. I pray that my children will emulate
You in this way.

May their eyes see the need in the world around
them. May their heart be moved with compassion for the
outcast, unwanted, unloved, neglected, orphaned, aged,
addicted, and homeless. Would You guide them to give
their time as well as their resources to providing kindness,
mercy, and relief to those in need?

Please help me set a good example for my children by
modeling a life of charity and compassion.

Amen.

Let no one despise your youth, instead, you should be an example to the believers in . . . love. – 1 Timothy 4:12

Lord of Love,

Your idea of love is radically different from the emotion our culture calls love. Your Word helps us see that real love is self-sacrificing service on behalf of others, regardless of the feeling or emotion.

I pray that my children will be wildly different from this world in the way they love. May their example be a beautiful display of Your humble service and how You continually cared more about others than about Yourself.

May their life be winsome and compelling in the way they emulate Your love.

Amen.

This is what love for God is:
to keep His commands. – 1 John 5:3

Lord of Truth and Wisdom,

The evidence of real faith is love—love for You, love for Your people, love for Your Word.

The evidence of love for Your Word is a desire to obey it. I pray this desire will be strong and real in the hearts of my children.

May it be, Lord, that my children so delight in Your Word that obedience is a joyful expression of their love for You. May it never be from a legalistic, grudging compliance but from a deep inner trust in Your wisdom and belief in the blessings that come to those who obey.

Amen.

Instruct them to do what is good, to be rich in good works,
to be generous, willing to share. ~ 1 Timothy 6:18

Our Generous God,

Whether or not my children ever have a lot of money that You entrust them to steward, they will have rich blessings because of Your presence in their lives. I pray they will be unselfish. Would You lead them to always care deeply about the needs of others and to be generous in responding to these needs?

Whatever they have, may they be willing to share with others. I pray that even from a young age, with siblings and with friends, may my children freely give what they have.

Though at times there will be those who take advantage of their generosity, may this not deter my children from being committed to being people who trust You with all that You entrust to them.

Amen.

If anyone thinks he is religious without controlling his
tongue, then his religion is useless and he deceives himself.
– James 1:26

Holy One,

My children's words will often be the clearest window
of what's going on in their souls. I pray that the overflow
of their lips will give proof of a soul that is right with You.

Would You convict my children of any lying, angry or
impure speech, and slanderous words? May they instead
by their words be a shining example of self-control. May
they choose to speak what brings life, hope, healing, and
give evidence of the authenticity of their faith.

May blessings come to them because of the
truthfulness of their words.

Amen.

Let us be concerned about one another in order to promote love and good works. – Hebrews 10:24

Our Great Hope,

We all need brothers and sisters to draw near to us as we walk this road of faith. Seeing the faith of others encourages us to stay strong.

I pray that my children will always have the blessing of dear members of the household of faith walking close beside them. May their example and influence guide my children further into a life of fruitfulness.

I ask also that my children will in turn have that same good influence on many other people. May they recognize the potential in others and help fan their gifts and talents into full flame. May my children's words be an encouragement to others to journey on with hope and strength.

Amen.

Always be ready to give a defense to anyone who asks you
for a reason for the hope that is in you. — 1 Peter 3:15

Hope of the Nations,

I pray that it is obvious that my children's lives are out of step with the dominant culture. I pray that their life causes others to wonder why they make the choices they do.

Whenever they are questioned about their faith, may they be prepared to give an answer. Would You meet them in those moments, whether they are formal or informal, with great clarity and conviction? May their tone of response be one of humility, gentleness, and care toward others while they are displaying a great reverence and regard for You.

May the hope within them be a shining light that draws others to who You are.

Amen.

I will be with you when you pass through the waters,
and when you pass through the rivers, they will not
overwhelm you. You will not be scorched when you walk
through the fire, and the flame will not burn you.
Isaiah 43:2.

Our Fortress,

The home You have designed for us in Your kingdom
will be a safe place. Until that time this world is not a safe
place. I care about many things in my life, but nothing
compares to how much I care for my children. When I
think about this big, frightening world they have to face, I
am tempted to worry. However, I will choose to trust You
and to continue praying for Your care and protection over
my children.

Through physical dangers keep them safe. In trials
and temptations hold them close. In peer pressure
strengthen them and let them not crumble. In suffering
may they not be overwhelmed.

Will You take all things the enemy intends for harm
in my children's lives and use them for good? They are
my precious children, God, and I trust them in Your care.

Amen.

Whenever you stand praying, if you have anything against anyone, forgive him, so that your Father in heaven will also forgive you your wrongdoing. – Mark 11:25

Our Faithful Forgiver,

I pray that my children will learn to develop times of prayer as sweet communion with You. May they come before You with an open heart willing to hear You speak to them of any sins or any compromise in their life.

As they are before You Lord, should You bring to mind someone with whom my children have an unreconciled relationship, may they be quick to do what it takes to make things right. May my children try not to go on with their lives holding bitterness or anger toward another. May unforgiveness never linger within their heart, and may they always show grace at the first opportunity.

Amen.

For those who live according to the flesh think about
the things of the flesh, but those who live according
to the Spirit, about the things of the Spirit. – Romans 8:5

Giver of Life,

Even after my children have committed their lives
to You, sin, though forgiven, will still dwell in their flesh.
They will struggle through all of their days. The desires of
their flesh will be at war against the desires of Your Spirit.

Most often the battle is won or lost in their mind. I
pray that my children will live with their thoughts set on
the priorities of Your kingdom. May their affections and
desires be for the things Your spirit desires to see happen
in the daily activities of their life.

Because of where their mind is set, may they daily
know life, joy, hope, peace, and victory.

Amen.

Trust in the LORD and do what is good;
dwell in the land and live securely. — Psalm 37:3

Lord,

I pray that Your name will be written across the hearts of my children. May they be sure of who You are. May they have great confidence that You reign over all things and are worthy of all of their life.

Out of that confidence may they live a life that is rich and overflowing with good deeds. May their heart be loving and kind toward all others they encounter.

Because they live to be a blessing to others, may they know Your rich blessings falling across every area of their life.

Amen.

Now to Him who is able to do above and beyond all that we ask or think according to the power that works in us.
– Ephesians 3:20

All-Powerful One,

You are perfect in power. Never have You had and never will You have more power than You do now. Never have You had and never will You have less power than You do now. All power is Yours. Your power gave us creation. Your power preserves and holds all things together. Your power accomplished salvation, and in power You will one day judge all people.

May my children trust in You as the Almighty One, and may their confidence in who You are give them great peace and hope. May they at times tremble before You in holy reverence—awed by Your greatness.

May it be great comfort to them that nothing is too hard for You—no prayer You cannot answer, no need You cannot meet, and no temptation You can't give them the strength to overcome.

Amen.

Be merciful, just as your Father
also is merciful. — Luke 6:36

Merciful Savior,

You withhold from us the punishment we deserve. You provide a way when we are helpless. You lavish Your mercy upon us. Your grace and forgiveness are never ending.

I pray that just as Your heart was moved, may my children's hearts be moved by those who are in need. Would You lead them not just to feel compassion, but may they take action to bring aid? For those in physical need, may my children take wise and helpful steps to lend a hand to the poor, the outcast, those orphaned and in distress.

More importantly, to those in spiritual need, some requiring a word of hope or encouragement, as well as others needing to hear the gospel, may my children speak words of truth that will be merciful and life-giving.

Amen.

I have come so that they may have life
and have it in abundance. – John 10:10

Life Giver,

Life with You is the deepest, richest experience anyone could hope for in the here and now and beyond. I desire this depth of blessing for my children.

With You as their Savior, may they drink deep of the spiritual riches that are theirs through Your grace— eternal life in Your blessed presence.

May they also know the overflow of that gift during their earthly days. May they know Your comfort, peace, hope, joy, strength, and love even this very day.

Amen.

He often withdrew to deserted
places and prayed. – Luke 5:16

God Who Draws Near,

Just as Your Son did during His earthly ministry, I pray that my children will be intentional in finding times of solitude. I ask that my children would never fear being alone but rather would enjoy it. I'm not asking that they would be loners—I want them to delight in being with people—but I'm asking that You would guide them to find a healthy, holy balance.

I pray that my children will know how to use their time well when they are alone. As young children, may they know how to entertain themselves. As they grow, will You help them value purity, and may they guard their minds, their lips, their ears, and what they set before their eyes when they are alone?

May they use times of solitude to draw near to You, seek after You, and find strength for what You have ahead for them.

Amen.

And Jesus increased . . . in favor with God — Luke 2:52

Giver and Builder of Our Faith,

I pray that our home and the years my children will spend here will be used by You to build a strong faith. May there be things along the way which require that our children will have to trust You. May they experience for themselves how faithful, kind, and good You are to Your children.

May they be diligent about being in Your Word as well as praying throughout the day. May they have opportunities to share what they are learning about You with other believers as well as chances to share Your good news with those who don't know You yet.

May their faith be active—always growing, always risking, always trusting.

Amen.

Why do you make me look at injustice? Why do you tolerate
wrongdoing? Destruction and violence are before me;
there is strife, and conflict abounds. – Habakkuk 1:3 NIV

Heaven's Holy One,

This world will assault my children's eyes with
immorality. The opportunities to look upon wrong will be
limitless. I pray that even when they are young, we will be
able to talk about this.

Would you help them believe in the value of purity?
Though in their flesh they will want to look at things they
should not, would you guide them to embrace the greater
treasure of holiness?

May they develop early the defenses they will need
to handle the countless moments when they encounter
temptation. Would you guide my children to experience
success in looking unto You and not upon the sinful things
of this world?

Amen.

Whoever wants to become great among you must
be your servant, and whoever wants to be first among
you must be a slave to all. — Mark 10:43–44

Our Great Servant Leader,

I pray that because of the strength of my children's
faith and convictions, and because of Your calling on their
lives, they will have the confidence to lead others. Yet I
ask that You would guide them to model their leadership
style after Yours.

May they view their role as that of a servant—always
showing others love, hope, and encouragement. Would
You help this to grow from a humble heart that never
considers themselves better than anyone else?

May their lives give evidence that they view others as
more important than themselves. May my children's care
and compassion for others create devotion that is willing
to follow after my children's leadership.

Amen.

All the days of the oppressed are miserable, but a cheerful heart has a continual feast. — Proverbs 15:15

God of Joy,

The sound of a child laughing is beautiful music to the heart of any parent. You desire for Your children to know deep joy, and I want the same for mine.

May my children be quick to laugh—not at things that are coarse, crude, worldly, or at the expense of others—but may they simply realize the humor in daily situations. May they experience often how laughter can create a quick bridge to a new or deeper friendship.

May they also not take themselves too seriously but be the first to laugh at their own foibles in a healthy, holy way.

Amen.

The one who follows instruction is on the path to life, but the one who rejects correction goes astray. — Proverbs 10:17

Giver of Wisdom from on High,

No discipline seems pleasant at the time—whether it comes from a parent, from a teacher, or from You, our heavenly Father. I pray asking that in times of discipline my children will know the heart of the one who is leading them and will trust that it is for their good. May they trust that it will ultimately take them to a place of blessing.

Would You guide them to seek after wisdom from those who lead them. May they not be led astray by the prideful hard-heartedness of others, and may they never be guilty of rejecting correction and leading others to do the same.

May they always have tender hearts longing for holy truth.

Amen.

A generous person will be enriched, and the one who gives
a drink of water will receive water. – Proverbs 11:25

Generous Giver of All Good Things,

I come today asking that You would lead my children
to see the reality that they have rich lives. Regardless of
the economics, my children will be loved and will know of
You and, therefore, their lives will be rich.

May my children always live openhanded with all the
resources they have. May they never have a clutching spirit
but instead be quick to share with others in need.

May they richly experience through all their days that
those who bless others will themselves be blessed.

Amen.

Let us be concerned about one another in order to promote love and good works, not staying away from our worship meetings, as some habitually do, but encouraging each other, and all the more as you see the day drawing near.
—Hebrews 10:24–25

Head of the Church,

I make this commitment to You Father that I will raise my children to attend church regularly. I pray that they will find so much life, joy, hope, and meaning from attending that they will always desire that type of fellowship for their entire life.

I realize a time will come when they will grow old enough to decide for themselves whether they wish to attend or not. I pray that being absent from fellowship will never be a pattern or habit in their lives.

In all seasons of their years, may they put themselves in places where they can worship You corporately, be exposed to the best Bible teaching available to them, and also serve You in the context of the local church. May my children truly love Your body, Your bride.

Amen.

I think of You as I lie on my bed. I meditate on You during the night watches. – Psalm 63:6

Our Peace and Joy,

I pray that my children will always sleep well—as young children, as teenagers, and as young adults. I pray that when they lie down it will be with pure hearts and with minds at rest. As they reflect on their day, may they see Your intimate involvement in all of their moments. As they lie awake, may they know Your nearness.

I ask that they never have to struggle with regular bad dreams or night terrors or sleeplessness. May their sleep instead be the rest of the righteous whose hearts and minds are set on You.

Amen.

I am not ashamed of the gospel, because it is God's power for salvation to everyone who believes. — Romans 1:16

Savior,

I pray that from a young age and throughout every moment they live may my children's hearts be captured by the glory of the gospel. May they first and foremost believe it and receive it for themselves. May they then always have a concern that those around them in their sphere of influence know of the salvation offered to them through trusting in Your atoning sacrifice on the cross.

Would You lead them always to be concerned for this message to go to all nations, and may they give of their resources to help make this happen?

Would they always have a strong confidence in the power of the gospel and the grace that is offered to all who trust in You?

Amen.

The one who reveals secrets is a constant gossip;
avoid someone with a big mouth. — Proverbs 20:19

Lover of Truth,

Our flesh is fascinated with hearing the latest bit of gossip. Yet in our spirits we feel the voice of Your Spirit convicting us and prompting us to walk away. I confess that often when I have heard the latest failure of someone else, it has led me in my prideful flesh to feel better about myself. This is wrong—I admit it, I repent of it and ask for Your forgiveness.

My children will have to deal with the same tension and struggle. May they turn to You, cry out for strength, and then resist the urge to be a part of slanderous talk.

May they also choose to be wary of those they hear spreading gossip about others, knowing they will spread gossip regarding them also.

May this type of sin never hold any lasting appeal to my children.

Amen.

Everyone who will acknowledge Me before men, I will also acknowledge him before My Father in heaven. But whoever denies Me before men, I will also deny him before My Father in heaven. – Matthew 10:32–33

One I Acknowledge as My Savior and Lord,

I come today asking that my children will have a bold and shameless faith. From the moment they first see their need for a Savior and cry out to You in repentance, may they desire for others to know they have placed their trust in You.

May they be bold in letting their family and friends know as well as their church family.

Throughout life may they be willing to quickly name Your name as the hope they hold. May they be unaffected by fear, worry, or pride from telling that You are their Lord.

Amen.

I prayed for this child, and the LORD has
granted me what I asked of him. — 1 Samuel 1:27 NIV

God Who Gives Good Gifts to His Children,

Being a parent at times is so much harder than I ever
imagined. I love it, but it tests me in ways I have not been
tested before.

In those times when I am in the deepest trenches
of parenting—exhaustion, stress, frustration, unrelenting
demands—let me not forget that my children are a sacred gift
from You. I asked for this gift, and You, my blessed Father, so
graciously gave them to me.

May this reminder of Your goodness to me refresh
and renew my soul even today.

Amen.

Love . . . believes all things, hopes all things.
– 1 Corinthians 13:6–7

God Who Is Glorious and Good,

I ask that as my children love other people, may they always believe for the best in them. Even as they will be disappointed at times, may my children still have hope for change and for a favorable outcome.

I pray that because they are so confident in Your sovereignty and certain that You are working in all things for good, may their attitude and disposition be one of optimism. May their bent be toward expecting the best out of others in all situations.

Will You guide them to trust that for themselves and for others, failure is never final because You are a God who redeems and restores? May my children never be considered cynical or suspicious.

Amen.

Be still and know that I am God. — Psalm 46:10 NIV

God Who Is Speaking,

This world is a loud place. Streets are filled with a steady rumble and roar. Rooms are filled with constant music, voices, and sound. Quiet is only found from intentionally seeking it.

I pray that my children will learn to treasure quiet, that they will know how in those moments to draw close and listen for Your voice. May they know what to do with a rainy afternoon or a lonely day that isn't crammed with activity.

In the silence, may they be at peace and be reminded of Your sovereignty and tender love.

Amen.

I pray that you may prosper in every way and be in good health physically just as you are spiritually. – 3 John 2

Lord God Strong and Mighty,

I pray today for the health of my children. I see clearly through the Old Testament laws regarding hygiene and dietary restrictions that You care about the well-being of Your people.

I ask that Your care, blessing, and protection would be over my children on all health fronts—physical, mental, emotional, psychological, and spiritual. Would You grant them wisdom in taking care of themselves? Would You guard and sustain them from attacks of the enemy on any of these fronts?

May nothing hinder them from the most fruitful service possible for You.

Amen.

"Repent," Peter said to them, "and be baptized, each of you, in the name of Jesus Christ." – Acts 2:38

One Who Has Washed My Sins Away,

When my children understand Your gospel and Your Spirit calling them to repentance, may they be quick to turn from sin and turn to You. May they trust in You and Your finished work on Calvary.

Also, may they at that time wish to be baptized. Would You have them desire to be identified with You in Your death, burial, and resurrection? I pray that this would be a significant and meaningful experience for them and the beginning of many moments of standing to proclaim You publicly as their Savior and Lord.

Amen.

Submitting to one another in the fear of Christ.
Wives, submit to your own husbands as to the Lord. . . .
Husbands, love your wives, just as Christ loved the church
and gave Himself for her. – Ephesians 5:21–22, 25

Cornerstone,

As my children look around this world of adult relationships, I ask that You would bless them with the privilege of seeing holy and healthy marriages. May they see examples in their family and in the lives of friends where the husband and wife truly love and serve one another.

May the relationships they see mark them with a godly ideal of what marriage should be. Would You allow them to witness faithfulness and commitment lived out as husbands and wives together seek You, Your guidance, and Your principles for life?

Lord, if You should have someone in Your plan to be the future spouse of each of my children, I pray that even today their lives are being blessed by some godly examples of marriage.

Amen.

For the eyes of Yahweh roam throughout the earth to show
Himself strong for those whose hearts are completely His.
– 2 Chronicles 16:9

All-Seeing One,

Not one tiny moment of someone's life goes unseen
by You. That You would behold every moment of every
life in every country through all time is mind-blowing!
We bow to Your omniscience.

Would You constantly find my children doing things
that are the actions of those whose hearts are fully Yours?
May their words and deeds reflect lives that are totally
caught up and surrendered to who You are.

As a result of this, may my children experience
powerful moments of Your presence. Would You grant
them at times words of wisdom that are beyond their own?
May they know the clear strong hand of Your protection.
Would You let them marvel at the way their lives are being
led and at how perfectly events are knit together by Your
wisdom and grace?

May knowing You in these powerful ways strengthen
their trust.

Amen.

The whole earth is filled with awe at your wonders;
where morning dawns, where evening fades,
you call forth songs of joy. — Psalm 65:8 NIV

One Who Will Forever Amaze Me,

Would You allow my children, through all of their days, to have a heart that can be captured by wonder? May they stand silent at a blazing sunset, fascinated by a waterfall, amazed at a starlit midnight, in awe of how a caterpillar crawls.

All of these great things are a trail of crumbs that lead the seeking to You, the Creator.

May these moments of wonder always lead my children to worship You.

Amen.

Love is patient, love is kind. — 1 Corinthians 13:4

Loving Lord,

May my children reflect You through a loving nature. I pray that their love would be patient. May they be willing to be inconvenienced or taken advantage of by others. Would You have them bear these times with no spirit of retaliation?

May my children be kind and willing to give anything to others. Would You have them always desire good for others and be active in working for it?

May this first and foremost show itself in relationships at home.

Amen.

The Lord is my light and my salvation—whom shall
I fear? The Lord is the stronghold of my life—
of whom should I be afraid? – Psalm 27:1

Our Fortress,

God, I ask that my children's trust in You will be a
shelter against fear. Would You have their faith to be so
confident in the fact that You are almighty, all-powerful,
and sovereign that many of the fears that beset other
people simply never cross my children's minds?

Even walking into strange new situations, would their
trust in Your nearness give them courage and confidence.
May their assurance of Your love give them a strong peace
as they rest at night.

Amen.

Better a poor man who lives with integrity than a rich man who distorts right and wrong. – Proverbs 28:6

Holy One,

You have heard me on countless occasions praying for blessings on my children. I understand that blessings come in many different forms.

While I do ask for financial provision to the degree that my children can handle it responsibly and honor You with it, more importantly I would ask that good things come to them as a result of living a life of integrity.

May their reputation be sterling. May they value it and guard it in all times of testing.

Amen.

My brothers, do not show favoritism as you hold on
to the faith in our glorious Lord Jesus Christ. — James 2:1

Perfect Judge,

God, we know You look upon the souls of all people.
You are not swayed in the slightest by pigment, prestige,
religion, or riches. One of Your attributes is Your perfect
impartiality.

I pray that my children would honor You by living
with a lack of favoritism or prejudice. May their assessment
of people not be based on looks, ethnicity, or social status
but instead see all as individuals in need of You.

Amen.

Be serious! Be alert! Your adversary the Devil is prowling around like a roaring lion, looking for anyone he can devour. Resist him and be firm in the faith. — 1 Peter 5:8–9

Lord of Hosts,

I am so grateful for Your great power, Almighty Lord. There is no other like You. You are able to defend us from any and all attacks.

Help me stay mindful and vigilant that a real enemy is looking for opportunities to come against my children. Some of these assaults will be direct, and some will be indirect.

May the belt of truth and the shield of faith guard and protect my children. May they believe sound doctrine and be quick to call upon You. Please strengthen them to stand firm and resist the enemy always.

Amen.

Honor your father and your mother so that
you may have a long life in the land that the
LORD your God is giving you. — Exodus 20:12

Our Father,

You are a God of order. You have designed this world to work through authority and submission. You have designed homes to operate in the same way. In the Old Testament the consequences to a habitually rebellious child were significant and severe.

I pray that seeds of pride will not flourish in the hearts of my children. As they relate to parents and other adults, may they display a humble spirit of love, trust, submission, and honor. In my children's lives may they be so convinced of my love and desire for their best that we avoid major episodes where this is even an issue.

For Your glory, may my children's desire always be to obey and honor their parents.

Amen.

If any of you lacks wisdom, he should ask God,
who gives to all generously and without criticizing,
and it will be given to him. — James 1:5

Giver of Wisdom,

No parent feels adequate for the task before them. It seems You use the work of raising children as one way to keep us aware of our dependence on You.

God, I declare my need for wisdom from You.

Thank You that Your Word gives us specific principles for successfully raising children. Would You guide me into the best books, the most God-honoring teaching available to know how to make specific application of these principles? Please keep my mind free of trendy, worldly philosophies regarding raising my children.

I desire to have the practical skills to parent with excellence. I come asking for Your wisdom and understanding.

Amen.

For if you forgive people their wrongdoing, your heavenly
Father will forgive you as well. But if you don't forgive
people, your Father will not forgive your wrongdoing.
— Matthew 6:14–15

Forgiving One,

Lord, I pray that once my children ask for Your
forgiveness for their sins, may the awe and wonder of Your
grace never fade from their lives. May they demonstrate
for all of their days that they are overwhelmed by the
mercy they have received.

In light of that wonder, may they never consider
withholding forgiveness from someone who wrongs them.

Because of Your grace, may they be quick to show
grace to every offender.

Amen.

As the One who called you is holy, you also are
to be holy in all your conduct. — 1 Peter 1:15

Holy One,

You have called us to be as You are. It is our heart's
desire to do that. Yet in this world none of us will ever do
it perfectly. We will try and we will fail.

You want Your people to reflect Your character. This
call and command rings clear in the Old Testament as well
as the New Testament.

I pray that my children will strive well to live holy
lives.

May they love the things that are pure and right in
this world and within themselves.

Would You let this world see Yourself reflected in my
child's life, priorities, and actions?

Amen.

Blessed are the meek, for they will inherit the earth.
– Matthew 5:5 NIV

Suffering Servant,

Into a world of people spiritually proud and self-sufficient in their good deeds, You came in a most unexpected and unimagined way. While You could have come in blazing glory and strength, You instead came as a humble lamb that would be led to slaughter.

Your meekness was not weakness, but it was great power that was perfectly controlled. May my children totally submit all of their power and energy to You. Violence and vengeance have no place in the lives of Your children.

You always lead with the purest wisdom as we choose to do Your will and not our own. May my child's strength and determination be used for Your glory.

Amen.

Coarse and foolish talking or crude joking are not suitable,
but rather giving thanks. – Ephesians 5:4

Our Redeemer,

So much of the humor of this world is based on
quickly turning an innocent phrase into one that is
slightly suggestive or even outright obscene. This is a
natural overflow of every heart given over to depravity
and immorality.

May this type of low humor be distasteful and
offensive to my child. May they laugh loud and often at
things that are wholesome but not at humor that involves
immorality and innuendo.

Thank You for the great joy You pour into the lives
of Your people.

Amen.

The fruit of the Spirit
is . . . faith. – Galatians 5:22

Faithful One,

You have never broken a promise. You have never failed us. Your Word is secure and worthy of our trust.

We are called to be like You in this way. I pray that the hearts and lives of my children will reflect a loyalty to You, to family, to friends, and to those who employ them.

May they also model a trustworthiness that is sure and dependable.

We rest in Your faithfulness, great God, and because of it we wait with confidence in Your return.

Amen.

Do not repay anyone evil for evil. Try to do what
is honorable in everyone's eyes. — Romans 12:17

Gracious God,

We see You on the cross forgiving those who nailed
You there. We will eternally stand in awe of this moment.
Clearly only supernatural power was able to accomplish
this.

I ask that Your power will flow through the life of my
children and they will not try to take vengeance on those
who hurt them. Please guide them not to speak ill of those
who offend them.

In their hearts may it be enough that You see all
situations and judge all events and people perfectly.

Amen.

You are to rise in the presence of the elderly
and honor the old. Fear your God. – Leviticus 19:32

Eternal God,

Pride blooms and shows itself in so many ways in our world today. One of the selfish ways it presents itself is through disrespect of the elderly.

I ask that my children will recognize that You have blessed some with a long life and many years. May their words and actions show a proper respect of the elderly.

May they always be attentive to and caring of older family members, friends of the family, and even strangers.

Amen.

The peacemakers are blessed, for they will
be called sons of God. – Matthew 5:9

Giver of Peace,

I ask that my children will live with the evidence of
hearts that are right before You. May this bring a deep,
abiding calm that is a strength and stability through all
their days.

From this place may it be a passion of their lives to
help others find peace with You.

May they live at peace with friends, siblings, and
others and even strive to help those around find peace in
their relationships.

Amen.

For the training of the body has a limited benefit,
but godliness is beneficial in every way, since it holds
promise for the present life and also for the life to come.
– 1 Timothy 4:8

Giver of Life,

So many things in this world are good in and of
themselves; yet someone will always exalt their importance
to a place beyond where they were intended to be. The
place of athletics and physical training occupies a place of
idolatry to many.

I do want my children, if they so desire, to be involved
in sports, training, and competition. Much good can be
derived from it—team fellowship, the quest of striving to
master a new skill, the joy of victory, and learning how to
handle defeat gracefully.

May my children have a right perspective on the
importance of athletics. May they always give more time
and attention to spiritual pursuits—cultivating a strong
prayer life, understanding Your Word, and loving service
to others.

May my children maintain a right balance of things
that are temporary and things that are eternal.

Amen.

Greet one another with a kiss of love. — 1 Peter 5:14

Loving Father,

I come today asking that our home would be one that is rich in affection. May my children see kisses and tender touches often among family members, and may these actives give them great confidence in the security and stability of our home.

May my children be quick with expressing appropriate affection with parents, siblings, and their friends. In a time when so many are starved for an arm around their shoulder, a reassuring hug, or a friendly kiss, may my children know the power they have to express care for others.

May it always be sincere, appropriate, and pure.

Amen.

Grow in the grace and knowledge of our
Lord and Savior Jesus Christ. – 2 Peter 3:18

God Who Is the Truth,

This world sends us a steady barrage of messages
moment by moment—some subtle, some overt.

I pray that my children will always be growing in
their knowledge of You in such a way that they are able to
discern clearly what messages from media are in harmony
with You and which are antagonistic to Your Word and
values.

May they develop great skill in rightly dividing truth
and half-truths and lies.

Amen.

Jesus increased . . . in favor with . . . people. — Luke 2:52

Triune God,

You are perfect in all the ways You relate to people. For those of us born into this broken world, it is a process of learning how to grow in grace and social skills.

I pray that my children will mature well socially. May they learn to relate to people of all age groups in ways that are respectful, caring, and appropriate. May their character earn them respect and admiration from those of all ages.

Would You guide them to always maintain a beautiful, simple childlikeness but never to be viewed as childish?

Amen.

I have treasured the words of His mouth
more than my daily food. — Job 23:12

God Who Is Not Silent,

I ask today that my children will always treasure Your Word. May they value the perfect and pure riches of Your self-revelation to us.

May they long to read it, hear it, learn it, memorize it, live it, and even teach it.

I pray that my life will say to them that I believe it is a holy treasure of unfathomable wealth.

Thank You for Your Word.

Amen.

Even when I go through the darkest valley,
I fear no danger, for You are with me; Your rod
and Your staff—they comfort me. – Psalm 23:4

Lord of Life,

At some point my children will encounter death for the first time. It may be with a favorite animal, a friend of the family, or perhaps a family member. They may be very young, teenagers, or even young adults when it happens for the first time, but it will be significant.

They will have questions. They will see sadness. They may even feel fear. I pray that the peace and hope we have from our relationship with You will be an extraordinary comfort to them in that time.

Would You even now prepare my children for that time by grounding them in Your truth about what happens at death? Would You guard their hearts and minds from abnormal fears anytime they think of it? Would You use any grieving experience in the lives of my children in ways that later bring You glory through their compassion shown toward others who grieve?

Amen.

I greatly rejoice in the LORD, I exult in my God.
– Isaiah 61:10

Giver of Joy,

I pray that Your joy will constantly overflow from my children. They will face difficult and trying circumstances along the way.

I ask that the pattern of their lives will not be ones of being sullen, moody, withdrawn, angry, distressed, or sad. These may be gray clouds, but would You have them to pass only briefly across the blue skies of their years.

May my children not base their outlook on life on whatever their current circumstances are. At best this would create brief periods of happiness. May they instead richly know the deeper and enduring joy that comes from a gaze that is constantly fixed on You.

Amen.

Be alert, stand firm in the faith, act like a man, be strong.
– 1 Corinthians 16:13

Almighty and Everlasting,

Throughout Scripture Your call and command went out, particularly to great leaders, to be strong and courageous. My children will surely face situations that will require great courage.

Would You prepare them now for that time? Would You guide them to learn the importance of keeping their eyes fixed on You instead of on the difficulties they are facing?

As they recall that You are almighty, all knowing, all powerful, all wise, faithful, holy, good, and sovereign, may it fan the flame of confidence within them to step into where You are leading them.

Amen.

Don't worry about tomorrow, because tomorrow will worry about itself. Each day has enough trouble of its own.
– Matthew 6:34

Our Omnipotent God,

Some people just seem prone to worry. Not only do they worry about the things of today, but they also worry about the possible things that could go wrong tomorrow.

I pray that this will not be true of my children. May they face their future, though it will be filled with many uncertainties, trusting that You are leading them into educational pursuits, relationships, and places of employment and service You have prepared for them.

May they be confident that Your mercies will be new each morning. May they trust that You will show them grace for that day and every day of their lives. May they find great peace and confidence in trusting that all of their tomorrows are already in Your hand.

Amen.

Our Lord and God, You are worthy to receive glory and
honor and power, because You have created all things, and
because of Your will they exist and were created.
— Revelation 4:11

Great Creator,

The first thing we know about You in all of Scripture
is that You are a Creator. From that first morning to this
morning, our world overflows with colors, sights, sounds,
and scents—countless things that show us how original
and inspired You are.

I know my children, created in Your image, will
have a creative side. It may show itself in different forms
throughout different seasons of their lives, but I pray
You will protect it. Guard it from voices that might seek
to make them discouraged and lose heart in their artistic
endeavors.

I pray that their artistic expressions will glorify You
and reflect to the world things that are good, pure, right,
and true . . . for Your glory.

Amen.

This is My body. . . . This is My blood. . . . I assure you:
I will no longer drink of the fruit of the vine
until that day when I drink it in a new way
in the kingdom of God. — Mark 14:22, 24–25

Lamb of God and Coming King,

I pray that every opportunity my children have to
partake in the Lord's Supper will be one they approach
with great anticipation, reverence, and respect. May they,
as You instructed us to, always examine themselves before
taking part (1 Cor. 11:25). May Your table continually be a
special and intimate moment of worship for them.

I pray that time at Your table will always move my
children to deep gratitude for Your great sacrifice on their
behalf.

I ask also that it will leave them with tremendous
hope and anticipation for those moments when, as
You promised, we will share the cup with You in Your
kingdom. What joy!

Amen.

The one who has My commands and keeps
them is the one who loves Me. – John 14:21

Worthy One,

You have heard me pray often that love might be a
rich and lavish overflow from my children's lives. May
their love for others be expressed through caring, sharing,
listening, giving affection, sacrifice, and speaking words of
truth and life.

When it comes to You, may their love be shown
through rich and deep worship and adoration. However,
most of all, if their love for You is in only one form, may
You see it consistently in their obedience of You. May
their trust in You, their love for Your Word, and their
desire to please You be reflected in how they quickly do
whatever You call them to do.

Would You lead them to make this their daily,
consistent offering of love to You?

Amen.

Now the Lord is the Spirit, and where the Spirit
of the Lord is, there is freedom. — 2 Corinthians 3:17

Giver of True Freedom,

I pray that my children will have the heart of a patriot. May they passionately love this land, defend it, want the best for it, and pray for its leaders. May they truly appreciate the high cost that has been paid by so many for the liberties we enjoy. May they always honor those who have sacrificed to secure and maintain our freedom. May they never take that freedom for granted.

Would You guide my children to always grow in their appreciation for the greater liberty You secured for Your people at the cross?

May their love and devotion for this nation be eclipsed only by their worship and adoration of You.

Amen.

Without faith it is impossible to please God, for the one who draws near to Him must believe that He exists and rewards those who seek Him. — Hebrews 11:6

The God We Will One Day See,

I pray that my children will truly trust and believe that though there are things we can't see, they are real nonetheless. May they have faith in the reality of Your kingdom where You reign even now over all things.

May they not simply believe in the existence of a divine being but that You, the God of all creation, the God of Holy Scripture, the One who had revealed Himself to us in Jesus, the God who reigns now in heaven and on earth are indeed the one true God.

May they believe that Your Son is the way, the truth, and the life; that Scripture is perfect and sufficient for all things; that their life has meaning and purpose; and that they will one day stand before You.

May my children experience the reward of those who seek passionately after You—forgiveness, righteousness, and heavenly blessings.

Amen.

On the first day of the week, each of you is to set
something aside and save in keeping with how he prospers.
— 1 Corinthians 16:2

Our Generous God,

I pray that my children always believe that every
penny they earn is actually a gift from You. May they also
realize that even though it is money in their hand, it in fact
still belongs to You.

From that right perspective, would You guide my
children to always be regular, willing, grateful, and joyful
givers? May they see all giving as a meaningful act of
worship to You.

Even from a young age, Lord, would You lead my
children to be faithful in stewarding the little they have
that You may one day entrust them with more?

Amen.

If you are offering your gift on the altar,
and there you remember that your brother
has something against you, leave your gift there
in front of the altar. First go and be reconciled
with your brother, and then come and offer your gift.
– Matthew 5:23–24

Our Reconciler,

I pray that my children will have a special sensitivity to the state of relationships. May they be aware when something is not quite right or is unresolved with a friend. May they never pretend or deny that things are out of sort. May they not try to go on with serving You while failing to give attention to the problem.

Whether the wrong is real or imagined, may my children be strong enough and humble enough to initiate toward the other person. I pray that through Your grace, they will be able to express what they feel and find mercy, understanding, and restoration. When this occurs, would You bless the relationship going forward and encourage both toward not letting relational wrongs go untended?

Amen.

A good name is to be chosen over great wealth;
favor is better than silver and gold. – Proverbs 22:1

Name Above All Names,

I pray that my children will care about having a good reputation among people. I ask this not that it may feed any fleshly pride within them; I ask that it may be a reflection of You in their lives.

I pray that there will be a long consistency of excellence in my children's lives. May this show itself in their work ethic, in their speech, in scholastic achievements, in their relationships, and in their self-discipline. May it cause people to take a closer look at my children's lives and want to see the motivation behind all they do.

May this always lead to chances to make You known.

Amen.

The fruit of the Spirit
is ... gentleness. – Galatians 5:22–23

Gentle Shepherd,

Everyone knows the tension and turmoil created from being around someone's child who is out of control. The unchecked lack of submission and defiance causes great uneasiness for those around.

I pray that my children will display a meek and gentle spirit. Though powerful and strong within, may my children's strength show itself in ways that are controlled and winsome.

Would You let the ease of their disposition create ease and enjoyment for those around them?

Amen.

Remember your Creator in the days of your youth:
Before the days of adversity come. — Ecclesiastes 12:1

The One Who Gives Life Meaning,

Youth can be a barrier that keeps some people from coming to You in faith. In youth so many temporal joys and distractions can keep people from asking the deeper questions of life.

I pray that my children will come to You at a young age. I ask that Your truth will arrest their hearts and gain my children's whole attention, focus, and devotion. Then with the most active and productive years ahead, they will have much opportunity to do work that gives glory to You.

In old age so many who don't trust You can be set in their loneliness and bitterness and held in the ache of an unfulfilled life. I pray that because my children have trusted You from a young age, their time as senior adults is peaceful, joyful, blessed, and still fruitful.

Amen.

Show family affection to one another with brotherly love.
Outdo one another in showing honor. — Romans 12:10

Heavenly Father,

The greatest outward evidence of someone being Yours is in the way they love others. I want our home to overflow with love. Today I come before You praying that my children will truly love one another.

May they be caring, giving, and compassionate toward one another. May affection be real and regular between them. May the bond they share be one they both cherish. Would You help them not just to see themselves as siblings but as truly dearest, closest friends? May their relationship reflect peace, kindness, and enjoyment of one another.

Would You help my children's lives to give evidence of not just sharing earthly parents but of also sharing a heavenly Father?

Amen.

Wisdom is supreme—so get wisdom. And whatever else you get, get understanding. — Proverbs 4:7

All Wise One,

No one accidentally becomes wise. For all who acquire wisdom, it is the ongoing, passionate pursuit of their lives.

I pray that my children, from an early age, will realize that some people live life in a way that seems smarter and better than the way others live. May they see that this blessing comes from following after Your instructions.

I pray that my children's hearts will be set to get wisdom. May it be a daily determination to chase after Your higher ways. May this passion for wisdom lead them not only deeper into Your Word, but may it drive them toward excellent authors and teachers and keep them away from much of the secular folly and drivel that passes for wisdom today.

Amen.

Live such good lives among the pagans that,
though they accuse you of doing wrong, they may
see your good deeds and glorify God. — 1 Peter 2:12 NIV

Holy and Perfect One,

I pray that my children will mirror You in their behavior. I ask that their example among unbelievers would draw attention. Even in discussions where someone may be speaking ill of another, I pray that they would turn to my children and say, "But you're different!" May the difference be the authenticity of the love and caring my children display for all people.

May they also project such a sense of joy and hope that it is appealing to others. May their lives be rich with deeds of love and humble service that nonbelievers will see an unbelievable difference in my children.

May they live for Your glory, and may their lives and reputation compel others to do the same.

Amen.

Do you see a man skilled in his work? He will stand in the presence of kings. He will not stand in the presence of unknown men. — Proverbs 22:29

God Who Leads Us,

I believe You have great dreams and plans ahead for my children. I believe You have in mind meaningful, purposeful work for them that will glorify Your name. I trust that You have uniquely designed them for this place of service and will call them to it.

May they seek after You diligently, listening for Your leading so they find work that is fulfilling and joyful. Please guide me now as I do what I can to equip them with character, skills, and values that will help them be excellent in the career path they choose.

Though I desire that their jobs will provide well for them, more than that I desire their work will be a way for them to join You in Your mission of redemption in this world.

Amen.

The LORD is good. – Nahum 1:7

Good and Gracious One,

You are good. In all You say, in all You do, You are good and perfect. In Your nature, in Your essence, You are good. All Your decrees, all Your creation—all is good!

May my children believe that they are indeed among Your good works that please You. May they also be aware of Your goodness to them in countless ways in this physical world—beauty, scents, colors, tastes, music. May my children live with deep and enduring gratitude to You for the good gift of salvation You have for them.

Would You guide my children constantly to respond to Your goodness with worship, faith, and adoration?

Amen.

Love your neighbor as yourself. — Mark 12:31

Lover of the Unworthy,

To truly love You we cannot have a heart that is aimed at You alone. To love You is to have that same love and care overflowing to any and all around us.

I ask today that my children will deeply, intentionally, and purposefully love the people they encounter. May their love not be simply emotional or sentimental, but may it be active in meeting the needs of others. May they give evidence of a helpful, caring, and compassionate spirit.

Would You guide them not to be selective or prejudiced with whom they will and will not love but truly be willing to love even those who may be considered enemies—just as You did with us?

Amen.

Don't stir up anger in your children, but bring them up in the training and instruction of the Lord. – Ephesians 6:4

Heavenly Father,

I ask for Your help that I may lead, train, and teach my children well without exasperating them. Please guide me never to punish out of anger but to see moments of rebelliousness as opportunities to instruct and train in wisdom.

May I never express anything that resembles favoritism among my children. I see from the biblical account of Esau and Jacob (Gen. 25:28) the devastating consequences of this.

Please guide me also that I may not set unrealistic expectations and push for achievement beyond reasonable limits. A child who bears this intense pressure will be crippled by feeling insufficient to ever please their overdriven parents.

I need You—Your Word, Your Spirit, Your wisdom—to do the job You have called me to do. Please lead me, fill me, and use me.

Amen.

At night I remember my music; I meditate in my heart,
and my spirit ponders. – Psalm 77:6

Faithful in All Seasons,

Though I would not wish it for my children, I accept
that in days ahead they will face times of trial, valleys of
loneliness, and dark nights when You seem to be distant. I
pray that in those times my children will remember well!

May they remember how faithful You have been in
all of life. May they remember how Your promises have
always proven to be true. May they remember that You
have never left them alone and always have had good
things ahead for them.

Would You lead their thoughts so that those
memories will provide them with comfort and strength to
endure the hard times?

Amen.

Never be lacking in zeal, but keep your spiritual fervor,
serving the Lord. – Romans 12:11 NIV

Our Intentional God,

Your Word instructs us that whatever we do, do it
with all of our might. I pray that my children will believe
passionately in whatever they take on to do, especially
spiritual pursuits.

May they wholeheartedly tackle the projects before
them and work with enthusiasm and attention given
to excellence. May they trust that You know and see all
things and that You care about details.

May my children's fervent spirit be a joy to their
instructors, and may their diligence inspire others around
them toward excellence. Would You guide them that they
would never be lazy or indifferent?

Amen.

When I kept silent, my bones became brittle from my
groaning all day long. . . . Then I acknowledged my sin to
You and did not conceal my iniquity. I said, "I will confess
my transgressions to the LORD," and You took away
the guilt of my sin. – Psalm 32:3, 5

Faithful Forgiver,

When my children sin, I want them to quickly feel
the weight of Your hand heavy upon their hearts. May
their spirits stay tender toward You so that the time of
conviction will quickly lead to their confession.

Thank You for the assurance of grace and forgiveness
whenever any of us confesses our faithlessness to You.
The certainty of Your love for us is such a kindness, and
Your kindness leads us to repentance.

May my children richly bless You for the mercy
and cleansing they find with You. May they never live
an extended period of time with guilt pressing down on
them.

Amen.

Iron sharpens iron, and one man
sharpens another. – Proverbs 27:17

Our Refiner,

While I pray that throughout their lives my children will always have good and godly companions, today I am petitioning for them to have faithful friends, particularly in the difficult years of middle school and high school.

I pray that You will bring a number of good friends their way but specifically that one best friend who will be a blessed and constant presence in my children's lives. I pray that the friendship will be mutually beneficial to both. May they encourage one another to be better people and more faithful to You.

May their conversations on intellectual or spiritual matters help them each develop sharper minds and a more certain faith. May the faithfulness of the relationship be a source of great comfort and joy to both of them.

Amen.

But you are a chosen race, a royal priesthood,
a holy nation, a people for His possession, so that you
may proclaim the praises of the One who called you out
of darkness into His marvelous light. — 1 Peter 2:9

God Who Defines Me,

I come asking today, in light of this passage, that my children will not see their identity in light of their accomplishments. Instead may they always view themselves as part of a chosen, holy priesthood belonging to You. May this define who they are and how they see themselves.

May they also live with an overwhelming awareness not only of the life You've called them to, but would You help them remember the life You've called them from? Would You allow this to keep a steady flame of joy and gratitude within their souls?

I want my children to be faithful in declaring Your praise. May they also declare You and Your truth to those who don't know You yet.

Amen.

Slaves, obey your human masters with fear and trembling, in
the sincerity of your heart, as to Christ. – Ephesians 6:5

God Who Is Present at All Times,

At some point my children will have their first jobs.
They will answer to someone other than a parent. I pray
they will be mindful that to serve an employer will be to
serve You well.

May my children demonstrate respect and obedience
to those in charge. May their diligence and their manners
win them favor with the ones they answer to. May they
be faithful to pursue excellence in all aspects of the work
they do.

Would You bless them, protect them, and guard
them concerning the influence of new people they will
begin to be around in their place of employment?

Amen.

Truthful lips endure forever, but a lying tongue,
only a moment. – Proverbs 12:19

One Who Is Truth,

All children are tempted to stretch the truth from time to time. Just like the first lie man told in Eden, it's usually to avoid consequence.

I pray today asking that the first few times my children tell a lie, may the consequences be such that they are convinced they don't want to lie anymore. I'm praying not simply for an outward compliance, but Lord, will You change their hearts? Would You help them see and believe that truth is the foundation for all good relationships?

As my children grow Lord, would they see how friendships based on truth telling are ones that endure.

Amen.

Ill-gotten gains do not profit anyone,
but righteousness rescues from death. — Proverbs 10:2

Giver of Good Things,

I know that at some point my children will be tempted to take shortcuts in doing the right thing. They may be tempted to cheat in some way or perhaps even steal. While I would wish for them to not give in, I pray that if they do, may it be something on a small scale, and may it happen while they are young. I ask also that the compromise would be revealed quickly, and may it be a great and memorable teaching opportunity.

Lord, would You use that time to impress upon my children the regret that comes when we take what isn't ours to take? Let them come away with the desire to not have it happen again. May they acknowledge that Your ways are better, higher, wiser, and always lead to a better life and blessings.

Amen.

Let no one despise your youth; instead, you should be an example to the believers in . . . conduct. — 1 Timothy 4:12

Giver of Life,

You not only gave us life, but You show us how to live it to the fullest. I pray that my children will value being a good example of one who is led by Your Word. May they make choices that reflect that You are their Lord.

I pray that the qualities they see in the example of Your earthly ministry will be ones they wish to emulate. Please protect and prevent them from ever living a hypocritical lifestyle of saying one thing with their lips and another with their choices.

May their life strongly emulate Your example here on earth.

Amen.

Just as you want others to do for you,
do the same for them. – Luke 6:31

The One Who Is Love,

I come asking that today's verse would be a guiding passage for my children's lives. May their general attitude toward everyone they encounter be one of asking, "How can I express love to them?"

May my children want to be known for being generous and caring and for always finding ways of expressing care toward people they are around. May they be quick to show sincere love in their words and through acts of service they initiate. May they be selfless and always focusing on the well-being of others with no thought to how they might be treated in return.

May my children be committed to expressing love even if others do not love them in return.

Amen.

Therefore, God's chosen ones, holy and loved,
put on . . . kindness. – Colossians 3:12

King of Compassion,

I want the evidence of Your character to shine in the lives of my children. A major way others will see Your image will be in the general kindness my children display.

May they truly be as concerned for the welfare of others as they are for themselves. May their kindness show itself in words and deeds of compassion.

Lord, Your kindness draws us to repentance. I pray that the kindness of my children will draw the best from others. May they be especially kind to their family and friends but also even to strangers they meet.

Amen.

Go, therefore, and make disciples of all nations,
baptizing them in the name of the Father and of the Son
and of the Holy Spirit, teaching them to observe everything
I have commanded you. And remember, I am with you
always, to the end of the age.' — Matthew 28:19–20

Immanuel,

I pray that my children will be disciple makers. May
their great passion be to see people come to faith and grow
into mature, fruitful, serving ministers. May my children
have a deep love for Your Word and for sharing its riches
with others.

At an appropriate time may there be someone my
children, as well as our family, has a burden to see come to
faith. May we be diligent to pray toward this end and to
speak truth as we have the opportunity. Would You then
allow us the privilege and joy of seeing this person come
to saving faith, and may the joy and the holy blessing of it
all so mark my children and be a significant part of their
story?

Thank You that as my children serve You, they can
have the confidence and certainty of Your presence with
them always. My children are Yours to use for Your glory.

Amen.

If you are ridiculed for the name of Christ, you are blessed,
because the Spirit of glory and of God rests on you.
— 1 Peter 4:14

Worthy One,

I have prayed often for my children to have a strong
and certain faith that will stand out of step with the
prevailing culture. I understand in praying for this that it
means at times some will dislike and wish to persecute my
children.

I pray in those times Lord that my children will find
the strength and grace to handle any insult or mistreatment.
May they faithfully endure and be protected and guarded
by Your hand. May Your Spirit fill them with power and
wisdom in those moments. May they boldly hold to and
proclaim their faith.

May they know the special blessing of Your approval
and satisfaction with them in those times.

Amen.

Give thanks in everything, for this is
God's will for you. — 1 Thessalonians 5:18

Sovereign One,

Your command is for us to give thanks in all things.
This is only possible if we trust that You are working
perfectly in the midst of all things—even the hard, trying,
and disappointing times.

I pray that my children will develop this kind of
heart of gratitude. I pray that I can see this type of
maturity in them and that they will be able to thank You
for the lessons You teach them in the midst of difficult
circumstances.

May they experience how You bring blessing out of
hardship. Make this increase their faith to trust You the
next time hard times come their way. Would You help my
children express their thanks to You even in the lonely,
sad, and uncertain seasons of life?

Amen.

Lord, I love the house where You dwell,
the place where Your glory resides. – Psalm 26:8

Head of the Church,

There is so much to love about Your church. It is the place Your Word is regularly, clearly proclaimed. It is where Your people gather to corporately worship and adore You. It is the one place where we meet to be mutually encouraged by fellow believers.

I pray that my children will love, like I do, everything about Your church. May they have great anticipation for our times of gathering with Your people. Would they look forward to the chance to worship You. Would You bless them with sincere and godly teachers and leaders along the way?

Would You give my children hearts of love for Your body, Lord?

Amen.

Praise the God and Father of our Lord Jesus Christ,
the Father of mercies and the God of all comfort.
He comforts us in all our affliction, so that we may be
able to comfort those who are in any kind of affliction,
through the comfort we ourselves receive from God.
— 2 Corinthians 1:3–4

Comforter,

Bless You for the Redeemer You are! You take the
hard times we go through and use them in ways that can
bring help to others. Amazing!

I pray that my children will indeed experience You as
their Comforter. In the midst of their hard times, lonely
times, sad times, and even moments of failure, may they
know Your nearness to them. May this give them strength
to endure and overcome.

Later, as they encounter friends who face similar
difficulties to what they've been through, may my children
be able to bless them through words and deeds that help
give strength and courage.

Amen.

Each person is tempted when he is drawn
away and enticed by his own evil desires. Then after desire
has conceived, it gives birth to sin, and when sin is fully
grown, it gives birth to death. — James 1:14–15

Tester of Our Faith,

I know You test our faith to see just how much we
really depend on You. You don't tempt us, but You do allow
the enemy to present us with temptations that are possible
for us to overcome through trusting and obeying You.

My children will have certain unique weaknesses that
the enemy will try to exploit. Whether these desires exist
through environment, upbringing, tendencies, or personal
choices, these are doorways through which temptation
will present itself. These temptations will always promise
something enjoyable when in fact they deliver something
harmful.

I pray that my children will be strong in the battles
they face. I pray that You will give them hearts that are
passionate about holiness and a love for honoring You
through purity. I pray that my children will be committed
to standing strong and always overcoming the opportunity
for evil at the earliest possible moment. Please help them.

Amen.

Therefore, God's chosen ones, . . . put on heartfelt compassion, . . . accepting one another and forgiving one another if anyone has a complaint against another. Just as the Lord has forgiven you, so you must also forgive.
— Colossians 3:12–13

Giver of Grace,

At some point friends will say things that hurt my children's feelings. Others will do things to cause them embarrassment or even harm. I pray that my children will be so confident in the grace they have been shown that they will feel no need to reciprocate. May they faithfully endure the wrong.

May the seeds of resentment never find a home within their hearts. May my children instead be quick to forgive and express it to the one who offended them.

Amen.

Unless the LORD builds a house, its builders
labor over it in vain. — Psalm 127:1

Perfect Father,

I desire for You to be intimately involved in every detail of the life of this family. I seek Your wisdom and leading for every area of our home life and relationships.

I declare my need for You and Your wisdom.

Jesus, will You be the foundation we all individually and united build our lives on? We want our family to endure—not just survive but to thrive and flourish more and more as years go by. This is only possible if we follow Your plans for how to "do life" and "do family" well.

Amen.

Speaking to one another in psalms, hymns,
and spiritual songs, singing and making music
from your heart to the Lord. – Ephesians 5:19

Giver of All Good Things,

I pray that music will have a special place in my
children's lives. Because of the joy and hope they have
found in You, I pray that their hearts will often overflow
with song. May it be the evidence of lives filled with Your
Spirit.

I pray that my children will be drawn to music that
is excellent and honoring to You. May they enjoy new
music that is excellent as well as high-quality music that
has endured through the centuries.

May they often sing to You in private as well as in
public. If they are interested, would You have playing
an instrument to be a rich and rewarding experience
for them? May it be a blessing to them and may they use
music to be a blessing to You.

Amen.

A fool gives full vent to his anger, but a wise man holds it in check. – Proverbs 29:11

Strength for the Weak,

It is a comfort to us that in Your Word we see You get angry. We get angry often. The difference however is that You are perfect, and we are not. We want Your strength and Your wisdom when times like these arise.

I pray that my children will exercise great self-control over how they express their anger. Please keep them from strong outbursts where they will say or do things they may later regret.

May they instead give careful consideration to what a godly response should be. May they own what they feel in situations where they are angry, but may they also express grace to the others involved.

Amen.

Your word is a lamp for my feet and a light on my path.
— Psalm 119:105

Light of the World,

You are the Great Shepherd that guides us through our days. You give us warnings to protect us from dangers, and You lead us into good places of blessing. Your Word shines truth on the road before us.

May my children love Your Word and in wisdom heed the warnings You give them. May this lead them to walk in ways that keep them far from sin. May they trust Your Word and the path it shows before them. Would You guide them to follow that light into ways of righteousness?

Because of a great passion for Your truth, may my children walk without stumbling.

Amen.

Therefore, since we are receiving a kingdom that cannot be shaken, let us hold on to grace. By it, we may serve God acceptably, with reverence and awe, for our God is a consuming fire. — Hebrews 12:28–29

God on High,

I pray that through conversations at home, Bible study, and all my children will absorb during their formative years, may they have high perspective of who You are. May they have a deep respect and reverence of You. May a healthy, holy fear color their days.

Please lead them to esteem You as the one true God that You are, the One who reigns from heaven with all power and authority and will one day powerfully, perfectly judge all people. Because of their high view of who You are, may it lead to a deep awe that You would even consider pursuing a relationship with them.

May this wonder and worship, along with the desire for intimacy with You, help keep them in a dear and growing relationship with You throughout their lives.

Amen.

For God loved the world in this way: He gave His One and Only Son, so that everyone who believes in Him will not perish but have eternal life. – John 3:16

Lord of Love,

Many things through life will try to tell my children what love is. Many books, movies, and songs will give them a skewed or even false definition of love.

I pray that my children will always look to Your sacrifice on the cross as the picture that forever defines for them what true love is. May they clearly see that You initiated relationship with us. May they be in wonder at the extent that You went to redeem us—laying down Your own life!

May this vision of self-sacrifice for the good of others be the ideal of love they strive to emulate with their own lives.

Amen.

If you do not do what is right, sin is crouching at the door. Its desire is for you, but you must rule over it. — Genesis 4:7

Strong Tower,

I pray that as my children grow in their faith that they will not be naïve about spiritual realities. May they come to understand that they have a real enemy who will try to thwart Your plans by bringing dishonor and even harm to them. May this reality not be something that frightens my children but instead motivates them to prayerfulness and sober, holy living.

May my children be convinced of the seriousness of even a small degree of evil or compromise. Would You have the metaphor of a roaring lion mark in them the reality and danger of the one who is their adversary?

May my children cry out to You with dependence, asking for strength to overcome the temptations set before them. May they regularly have moments of victory that bring You great glory.

Amen.

What it is the LORD requires of you: to act justly, to love
faithfulness, and to walk humbly with your God.
– Micah 6:8

God of Justice,

Everything You do is perfect and right. We cry out
for Your kingdom to come because we long for a time
when there will be no injustice and everything will be as
it should be.

I pray that my children will have a heart of mercy
for the downtrodden of this world. May they care deeply
about the poor and afflicted as well as for orphans and
widows. May they give time to bringing relief and aid to
them.

May my children live their days with a humble heart
as they walk through this world in right relationship with
You and with others.

Amen.

Don't worry about anything, but in everything, through prayer and petition with thanksgiving, let your requests be made known to God. – Philippians 4:6

God Who Is Near,

There will be times when a wave of worry will wash over my children—an upcoming test, a big sports game, a new and uncomfortable situation they find themselves in. I pray that You and I will have adequately prepared them to handle such moments.

May they trust that You have led them *to* that moment and that You will lead them *through* that moment. May they focus their attention on Your sovereignty and Your power. As happens whenever we have a high opinion of who You are, would You allow peace to reign in their hearts and minds?

In these moments may they be quick to run to You and pour out their concerns.

Amen.

I will bring you health and will heal you of your wounds—
this is the LORD's declaration. — Jeremiah 30:17

Healer,

In every childhood there will be times of sickness or disease. While I may wish this were not true for my child, I do trust that You will build up their immunity.

In the times when my children are sick, Lord, I pray that it will be nothing too severe. May You lead us to find excellent medical help, and may my children be wise in getting rest and taking their medicine. May You guide them to have pleasant experiences with doctors, nurses, and dentists and not to be fearful of them.

Even as health is restored through a doctor's care, we will acknowledge Your good hand, for only You can truly bring healing. Bless You.

Amen.

Know that Yahweh your God is God, the faithful God
who keeps His gracious covenant loyalty for a thousand
generations with those who love Him and keep His
commands. — Deuteronomy 7:9

Faithful One,

You are gloriously perfect in Your attribute of
faithfulness. In a world where in business and relationships
there is overwhelming evidence that for many people
their word is not their bond, You are always completely
true to Your Word. Your Holy Book is a catalog of stories
where You were beautifully faithful to Your word and
Your people.

I pray that this will stir great confidence in the hearts
of my children. May it lead them to ever-increasing faith in
the trustworthiness of Your Word. May they cling tightly
to the certainty of the fulfillment of all Your promises.

Amen.

And Jesus increased in ... stature. – Luke 2:52

The One Who Knit Us Together,

It is amazing that Your Holy Word includes a verse regarding how Jesus physically grew. I pray for healthy growth for my children as well.

May all of their senses, systems, and faculties develop well and appropriately. May their minds be sharp and clear. Would You give them a love for physical activity and recreation as well as for making healthy nutritional choices?

Would You protect them from any way the enemy may plan to sabotage their physical health and growth? May their bodies serve them well as they serve You.

Amen.

Run from sexual immorality!
— 1 Corinthians 6:18

Wise and Holy One,

I ask that even from a young age, will You lead my children to make wise decisions about guarding their sexual purity. May they be committed to Your ideal of the incredible gift of sex belonging only within the context of marriage.

May they set strong boundaries that will guard their bodies as well as their minds and spirits. Would You meet and sustain them mightily in all moments of temptation?

May they be strong and secure enough in themselves, and in Your love and my love, that no opportunity to give themselves away before marriage seems worth it to them.

Please keep them safe from any perversion or predator that might be a part of the enemy's plan for my children. May any attack of this manner be totally crushed before it can even present itself.

May they experience in marriage the rich blessing of deep intimacy in sex that is a reward for the wisdom of their early choice for purity.

Amen.

The fruit of righteousness is sown in peace
by those who cultivate peace. – James 3:18

Our True Peace,

I pray that my children will be sensitive to relational
tension between themselves and others and will be the
ones who want to be a peacemaker. May they be well
respected and trusted so that others feel safe telling my
children what's really going on and what has caused the
problem.

Would You guide my children in these times with
great wisdom, and may they faithfully seek Your counsel?
May they be able to help others find a grace-filled solution.

I ask that even in their youth, may this be a role my
children will exercise in relationships with siblings and
friends.

Amen.

Therefore, since we also have such a large cloud
of witnesses surrounding us, let . . . us run with endurance
the race that lies before us. – Hebrews 12:1

Author and Perfecter of Our Faith,

I pray that my children will have a strong and determined spirit—almost stubborn and unmovable when they know that the cause is right.

I pray that as it relates to their faith, they will be ever in forward motion. Even though at times they will stumble and make mistakes, through their failures and compromises, may they gain great wisdom and strategies for how to avoid a similar failure next time. Because of what is gained, even when they fall, may they be falling forward.

May they be determined to press on, forgetting what lies behind, never slowing down and never giving up.

Amen.

His delight is in the LORD's instruction,
and he meditates on it day and night. — Psalm 1:2

Living Word,

I know the priority You place on Your people spending time in Your Word. I agree about its importance. I want my children to delight in reading Your Word. Today I come before You asking that You will help them to be good readers.

May they always love books, reading, and learning. If at some point for some reason, they find reading difficult, would You guide me to find the help they need? I ask that any periods of difficulty with reading will only be short-term seasons that they eventually overcome and then catch up and even go beyond whatever the skill level for their age is supposed to be.

The brain—and how we learn—is a wondrous, miraculous part of Your design. Would You guide my child to be excellent in reading?

Amen.

Therefore, brothers, by the mercies of God, I urge you
to present your bodies as a living sacrifice, holy and pleasing
to God; this is your spiritual worship. — Romans 12:1

Worthy One,

There will be times in worshipping You that my
children will offer up a prayer. Other times they may offer
a song, a word of praise, or even bring their tithes and
offerings to You. Of all they will ever offer, I pray that
first and foremost they will offer themselves to You—all
that they are: body, mind, emotion, and will.

In light of who You are and the countless,
indescribable mercies You have shown them, this will be
a reasonable and right response on their part. May they
daily offer themselves to You to use in any way that You
desire.

May they see incredible, fruitful things happen
in their lives, and may these things give evidence and
encouragement that You are indeed Lord of all of them.
For Your glory always Lord.

Amen.

The fruit of the righteous
is a tree of life. — Proverbs 11:30

The God Who Seeks and Saves,

I pray that my children will live with an awareness
that people around them every day are looking for answers
for the difficulties they face and for the meaning of their
lives. May they take advantage of the opportunities they
have to speak of the hope they have found in You.

I pray that they will actively prepare themselves for
any chances they have to share the gospel.

May there be those who are in heaven one day
because of Your Spirit moving through the influence of
my children. May Your mission be my children's mission.

Amen.

It is more blessed to give than to receive. – Acts 20:35

Our Provider,

Everything we have has come from You. You are so gracious and lavish in the way you treat Your children. It is our desire to be like You.

I pray that my children will be faithful in stewarding all You give to them. May they be unselfish and generous in every opportunity they have to care for others. I ask that their lives would be rich with the blessings that come to those who give freely to others.

May they live with eyes that are always on the lookout for opportunities to give to others.

Amen.

David said to the Philistine: "You come against me with a dagger, spear, and sword, but I come against you in the name of Yahweh of Hosts, the God of Israel's armies."
— 1 Samuel 17:45

Name Above All Names,

My children will be called to fight some battles. Some may simply be struggles against some difficulty they face; others may be to oppose something that opposes You.

In those moments, Lord, may my children never feel they are taking on the battle alone. May they be sure of Your nearness. May their faith triumph over any fear they feel. Would You guide them to experience how weapons of the enemy are no match for Your powerful name?

May my children be sure of their right relationship with You and then proceed with confidence in Your mighty power.

Amen.

You must not bring any abhorrent thing into your house, or you will be set apart for destruction like it. You are to utterly detest and abhor it, because it is set apart for destruction.
– Deuteronomy 7:26

Our Fortress,

Like most families we will struggle with what media influences to allow in our house. We cry out that we will need Your supernatural guidance to help us make wise decisions regarding what will have an effect on our children. Please lead us.

Lord, I also pray about the books, movies, games, music, and clothes my children will bring into our home. Please guide them that they will not want to bring in anything impure or dishonoring to You. Father, if they should, please guide me with discernment to help discover it that it might be removed. Should that occur, I pray that You will lead us into a grace-filled time of teaching and that my children will respond well with a tender, compliant spirit. May they also desire for the offensive item to be removed. Please lead them to not develop a taste for worldly things in media choices.

May it be the declaration of everyone in our house that we will set no evil thing before our eyes.

Amen.

We must not become conceited, provoking one another,
envying one another. — Galatians 5:26

Mighty King,

You hear me asking often for good things in my children's future—rich blessings, fruitfulness, and success. I am aware that each success, whether it's academic, athletic, artistic, or even spiritual provides the enemy with an opportunity to slip in and tempt my children with pride.

I pray asking that my children will not give in to the temptation to be prideful. May they instead in gratitude bless You as the Giver of every good thing that comes their way.

May they always model a humble spirit that is beautiful and attractive to many. May You be glorified in their successes as well as in the praise they give You for their successes.

Amen.

Do everything without grumbling and arguing.
Philippians 2:14

Our Provider,

We live in a land and time that regardless of social class it puts us among the most resourced and blessed in all the history of humankind. And yet we are arguably among the most discontent people also.

I pray this will not be true of my children. May they realize that whatever their status (professionally, financially, socially) in life, it is one You have allowed. May my children never have a critical or ungrateful spirit but trust in Your will and provision for them.

May their faith in You keep them from grumbling and complaining.

Amen.

A generous person will be blessed, for he shares
his food with the poor. — Proverbs 22:9

God Who Gave Us His Best,

The majority of people go through their day looking
for what can benefit them. Their eyes are set on what they
can get out of life. I pray that my children will live with
their daily focus being on what they can give to others.

May they go through their day seeking out
opportunities to be a blessing to others, whether through
a kind word or through some deed that answers a real
need.

I trust fully that if my children live this way, Your rich
blessings will overflow back onto their lives.

Amen.

How good and pleasant it is when brothers
live together in harmony. — Psalm 133:1

God of Truth and Peace,

On a physical, relational level, I pray that there will
be unity between my children and their siblings. May they
respect, love, and truly care for one another, and may it
result in a sweet peaceful life for all.

I pray also that my children will find like-hearted
and like-minded friends. May they develop a tight and
caring bond of faithfulness.

On a spiritual level I ask that throughout life, Your
Spirit would guide my children into relationships with
other believers who will be their brothers and sisters in
the faith. May these relationships be built on a deep love
for You and Your Word. May the beauty and peace of
these relationships be examples to others of the blessing
that comes when You are the center of a friendship.

Amen.

The fruit of the Spirit is . . . goodness. – Galatians 5:22

Good Shepherd,

In many instances these days, it seems that referring to someone as "good" is almost a term of derision or a put-down. It is simply not a quality that is celebrated much.

Lord, I desire that my children would care deeply about all things that are morally and spiritually excellent. May they value things that are of the highest standard, and may that shine the beauty of Your character.

May Your goodness follow my children all the days of their lives.

Amen.

I will hasten and not delay to obey your commands.
Psalm 119:60 NIV

God Who Does All He Says He Will Do,

I pray that my children will reflect Your character in their diligence. So many people are filled with good intentions but never seem to get around to doing what they say they will do. May my children learn the wisdom in doing quickly what they set their minds to do. May they experience the blessings that come to people who live this way.

Especially in relation to serving You, may they not delay in obeying the instructions they find in Your Word. As Your Spirit prompts their hearts at times, may they move soon to carry out what You desire for them to do.

May my children not be seen by You or by others as a procrastinator.

Amen.

Finally, all of you should be like-minded and sympathetic,
should love believers, and be compassionate and humble.
— 1 Peter 3:8

God of Compassion,

You've been so lavish in the mercy You have shown us. You saw us as poor and in need and responded with what we needed most—a Savior.

I pray that my children will have tender and compassionate hearts. May they identify with the lost and the least. May they be moved to respond in a sweet, humble manner showing love just as You would.

Please guard this tender place within them. Even if people should take advantage of their kindness, will You keep them from becoming cynical and hard-hearted? May they continue to reach out as Your hands in this world.

Amen.

So then, each of us will give an account of himself to God.
– Romans 14:12

Our Foundation,

As my children come to understand Your Word, may they become aware of the reality that one day all who call on You in faith will stand before You to give an account of their life. This will not be a judgment of punishment for sin (that was settled at the cross) but instead an evaluation of the quality of work done during their lifetime.

I pray that my children will desire to do excellent work that brings You honor.

May their conduct here on earth, as well as their service to You, be excellent. May they use the spiritual gifts You have given them. May their lives and their labor result in works that are built of gold and silver and not hay and straw. Please guide the fruit of their lives to survive and stand strong through the fire of Your inspection.

Amen.

I will never leave you or forsake you. – Hebrews 13:5

Our Ever Present Help,

I can trust my children in Your care because there will never be a moment when You, the all-powerful One, will not be as close as their next breath. Whatever the situation in life, may this truth be a great source of comfort for them.

Especially in any season when they are dealing with loneliness or feeling abandoned by a friend, may they turn to You and be strengthened by Your faithful nearness.

If there are moments when my children feel fearful, please remind them of the closeness of Your presence to them, and may they find peace.

Amen.

I am teaching you the way of wisdom;
I am guiding you on straight paths. — Proverbs 4:11

Our Great Teacher,

Throughout childhood and the teen years, my children will spend so much time in educational settings being prepared for what You have ahead for them to do. In those settings they will be exposed to a wide variety of people with different backgrounds, beliefs, and priorities.

Through the process I pray that You will:

Use the influence of their instructors to help them grow in knowledge and wisdom.

Guard them from ungodly ideas and influences.

Guide them to be certain of what they believe to be true about You and to articulate their belief clearly.

Keep them safe and growing in mind, body, and spirit.

Amen.

LORD, reveal to me the end of my life and the number of my days. Let me know how short-lived I am. — Psalm 39:4

Eternal One,

However many days we walk this earth, it is brief in the light of eternity. I pray that because of Your Word of truth being poured into my children, may they live with the wise assessment that life is fleeting.

Because of this perspective, may my children be passionate and motivated in the work they do. May they not be prone to waste time.

Would You lead them to live being kingdom minded? May they be wise in choosing how they spend their time. May they always let their love be spoken.

Amen.

We are pressured in every way but not crushed; we are
perplexed but not in despair; we are persecuted but not
abandoned; we are struck down but not destroyed.
— 2 Corinthians 4:8–9

Almighty One,

My children will be subject to many frustrations
throughout their lives. Many of these will come because
of their limitations and weaknesses. This is all a part of
Your perfect design. Through frail and faulty people You
move and work to bear testimony to the nations of Your
great power.

I pray that my children will have great confidence in
Your strength in the midst of whatever they are facing.
May they be sure they can endure anything by Your
power. Would You help them feel they are never alone in
trials, and may they always know the close companionship
of peace and hope?

May they find that all of their trials, and even their
humiliations, are a chance for Your sustaining power to
shine before the world.

Amen.

You must not follow a crowd
in wrongdoing. – Exodus 23:2

Savior and Lord,

Every child feels the temptation to follow others
in doing wrong. We all know well that wave of fear that
washes over a heart at the point where we have to consider
if we will dare to stand opposed to what the majority is
doing.

I pray that my children will develop at a young age
the strength of character to stand on their own in doing
what is right.

May their example of being willing to stand alone
inspire others to also resist evil, even when "everybody
else is doing it."

Amen.

Don't be led astray by various kinds of strange teachings.
– Hebrews 13:9

God of All Truth,

I feel that the desire behind so many of my prayers is for my children to be deeply, deeply rooted in Your powerful and Holy Word. I know that throughout their lives they will encounter strange and heretical spiritual teachings. Some may even come from popular teachers. Others may come from those who once seemed biblical and orthodox.

May my children know real truth so well that they are able to discern the false when it comes along. May they always run back to Your Word to see what You have to say whenever they face a suspicious teaching.

May their love of truth bear much fruit that honors You.

Amen.

A tranquil heart is life to the body, but jealousy
is rottenness to the bones. – Proverbs 14:30

Provider of All We Need,

I believe through every season of life, You will be
faithful to provide all my children need. Please lead them
to believe this to be true and to be content with what You
provide. May they always remove the seeds of discontent
that fall onto the soil of their soul long before they can
ever bloom into full jealousy. May they be satisfied by their
relationship with You.

Also in this verse, Lord, I see the relationship
between what's going on inside the body and how it shows
itself on the outside. I pray that my children will pursue
wisdom, purity, and holiness and that it will be reflected in
a good healthy quality of life and a strong mind and body.

Amen.

Take delight in the LORD, and He will give
you your heart's desires. — Psalm 37:4

Our Light and Our Guide,

I come before You today asking that You would
guide my children to fully and always find their delight
in You. By that I'm asking that they may find all their life,
their joy, their hope, and their purpose in You. May You
be their center and focus as well as the great consuming
passion of their lives.

If that is the case, You have said You will put within
them desires that are good, right, and holy. As my children
look ahead at their future, I pray they will feel freedom to
pursue these desires that are within their hearts.

May they find life to be a joyous adventure as they go
after their dreams.

Amen.

Love your enemies and pray for those
who persecute you. — Matthew 5:44

God of Grace,

Though I can't believe my children will ever set out to make enemies, because of the broken world we live in, some people for whatever reason will simply wish to bring harm to them.

I pray that my children will have such faith in Your ultimate perfect judgment of all people that they will feel free to leave the judgment up to You. May they obey Your command and simply concern themselves with how to show love to people.

Would You bring to my children's minds the thought of considering the spiritual state of those who persecute them? May they choose to pray that their enemies will repent of their wrong deeds and seek reconciliation with You and with them.

Amen.

The LORD gives, and the LORD takes away.
Praise the name of Yahweh.   Job 1:21

God over All,

Sometimes life will break my children's hearts, and watching that happen will break mine. Like everyone, they will sometimes experience deep sorrow and loss.

While I pray for comfort on many fronts in that time (Your nearness, Your Spirit, godly friends), I pray that my children will fall hard on Your sovereignty and believe that You are active in their lives, even in those crushing moments. May they trust You, though it is hard. May they worship You, though with tears in their eyes. May they believe that You have allowed this disappointment to happen and that even in the midst of it, You are good and wise. May they rise up, even when filled with sadness, and still bless Your name.

Amen.

I will never leave you or forsake you. – Hebrews 13:5

Our Constant Companion,

At moments throughout life, my children will feel the pangs of loneliness. It may be a time of being deserted or forsaken by a friend, or it may simply be learning how to handle a few hours of solitude.

In either case may they be certain of Your nearness to them in those times. May they find great comfort in the pledge throughout Your Word that you will never leave or forsake them.

Would You have the promise of Your constant presence to be a strength that empowers my children to press on through all of the trying times of their lives?

Amen.

So if I, your Lord and Teacher, have washed your feet,
you also ought to wash one another's feet. — John 13:14

Our Loving Example,

Most of the prayers I pray for my children are so
they will live a life that brings You honor and brings them
blessing. One of the most certain ways of ensuring this is
for them to live in ways that reflect Your love. Your Word
helps us see that the essence of true love is self-sacrifice.

I ask that my children will have an attitude of
humility and service to others. May they look around for
opportunities, just as You did, to meet real needs. May
they strive to put the interests of others ahead of their
own. Always for Your glory, Lord.

Amen.

Just as you don't know the path of the wind, or how bones
develop in the womb of a pregnant woman, so you don't
know the work of God who makes everything.
– Ecclesiastes 11:5

The Incomprehensible One,

I pray that there will be times when either Your
Word, a sermon, or some other book about You will
simply leave my children overwhelmed by how beyond
understanding You are. May there be times when they
pause to ponder how inconceivable You are to the limited,
finite, human mind. May they be lost in divine, holy
wonder as they adore You.

Would You lead them to consider Your vastness,
Your infinitude, and Your all-sufficiency? May it humble
them to realize that even with a lifetime of studying
You, they are simply scratching the surface of the great,
inexhaustible truth and love that You are. May they be in
awe that though many will know You as a consuming fire,
they will know You as a tender Father.

May the holy, unknowable mystery of You lead them
to great reverence, humility, and trust.

Amen.

I tell you that on the day of judgment people will
have to account for every careless word they speak. For
by your words you will be acquitted, and by your words
you will be condemned. — Matthew 12:36–37

God of All Purity and Wisdom,

I come today asking that my children will live with
an awareness of the weight of their words. May they see
that their words are like stones that can be thrown to do
incredible damage or be used to build something fantastic.

May they feel the responsibility of using them wisely
as their words are one of the most sure evidences of the
reality of their spiritual state.

May they stay away from words that are deceitful,
destructive, foolish, proud, or vulgar. May they be careful
to strive to always speak the truth in love as You have
called them to do.

Amen.

Finalize plans with counsel. — Proverbs 20:18

Light for Our Journey,

I come today, Lord, interceding on behalf of my children regarding the big decisions they will have to make in life. As they approach the second half of their teen years, choices regarding college and work will loom large. They will face decisions regarding deepening relationships with members of the opposite sex. They will wrestle with discerning Your will and Your call on their lives.

In these important matters and so many others, I pray that they will seek out and listen to wise counsel. May their hearts be set on finding out not what is simply good but what is better and even best.

Will You consistently meet them through Your Word and through the advice given to them from godly leaders and friends?

Amen.

If . . . My people who are called by My name humble
themselves, pray and seek My face, and turn from their
evil ways, then I will hear from heaven, forgive their sin,
and heal their land. – 2 Chronicles 7:13–14

Giver of Grace,

I pray that my children, as they grow, will care deeply
about the spiritual condition of our nation.

May they pray for their political leaders as You call
them to do. May they ask that our freedoms and liberties
be opportunities we use to physically and spiritually bless
others.

As they see policies, leaders, and agendas that bring
dishonor to You, would You lead them to pray for revival in
the heart of this nation? May they be moved to intercede,
knowing that the only real hope for any individual or
people is through humility, prayer, repentance, and
longing for You.

Amen.

I know the One I have believed in and
am persuaded that He is able to guard what has been
entrusted to me until that day. — 2 Timothy 1:12

Faithful God,

People and things will disappoint my children. People will make and break promises. "Love" will turn out to be temporary and conditional.

However, when it comes to You, may my children be so convinced of the truthfulness of Your promises that it gives them great assurance.

May they have such confidence in who You are and the reality of Your coming kingdom that they live with a holy strength and boldness.

Amen.

Set your minds on what is above,
not on what is on the earth. — Colossians 3:2

Lord of Heaven and Earth,

I pray that my children will come to understand that through saving faith they are indeed citizens of heaven. Even though their feet will walk in this world, may their minds and thoughts be on Your kingdom.

May the tension of a world that they are *in* but not *of* lead them to look at all of life through the lens of eternity. Would You guide them to make wise decisions after considering the long-term, eternal perspective? May they value the things of heaven more than the things of earth.

Amen.

Patience is better than power, and controlling
one's temper, than capturing a city. — Proverbs 16:32

Prince of Peace,

I pray that my children will see the incredible
blessing that comes to those who can control their temper.
May they believe that self-control is a great strength and
of far greater value than any worldly success.

May they choose to be patient and trusting even
when they are frustrated by not getting what they want.

I understand that more than anything I ever say
about this virtue to my children, my greatest influence will
be in seeing it modeled in my life. Lord, please help me set
an example of one who restrains anger.

Amen.

Be gracious to me, Lord, because I am in distress; my eyes
are worn out from angry sorrow—my whole being as well.
– Psalm 31:9

Comforter,

I pray that my children will know You well as the
source of the greatest joy of their lives. May they see Your
good hand behind every blessing that comes their way.

May they also know You well, and perhaps even more
intimately, in the times of sorrow they face. On days when
they feel alone, disappointed, or rejected, help them call
on You and draw near to You. They will find You to be the
Faithful One who never disappoints. May they know Your
comfort and the nearness of Your presence.

Would You always use sadness and solitude to draw
them close to You?

Amen.

Do not be deceived: "Bad company corrupts good morals."
— 1 Corinthians 15:33

Wise and Faithful Friend,

I know I will prefer my children not spend much time with some of their peers. I can't control which people my children will be exposed to, but, Lord, You can control which friendships form.

I pray that the peers my children find attractive would be ones that share common values. May my children simply not allow those that would be a bad influence to have the opportunity to speak into their lives.

May Your Holy Spirit draw near giving them wisdom on whom to be friends with and whom to avoid.

Amen.

Solid food is for the mature—for those whose senses
have been trained to distinguish between good and evil.
— Hebrews 5:14

Our Master and Teacher,

Just as I hope to see my children grow up and mature
physically and mentally, I also desire to see them mature
spiritually. I've prayed often that they will be drawn to
Your Word.

May my children not simply hear Your truth but
willingly put into practice all that You command them to
do.

May they have an attraction to the deeper truths of
Your Word. May they, at an appropriate time, begin to
leave the milk of elementary teaching and acquire a taste
for the meat of doctrine and theology. I ask this, not that
it would ever lead to any pride on their part but that it
would lead to greater fruitfulness from their lives for Your
glory.

Amen.

We cared so much for you that we were pleased to share with you not only the gospel of God but also our own lives, because you had become dear to us. — 1 Thessalonians 2:8

Shepherd of the Saints,

I will strive to teach, train, and prepare my children for what lies ahead for them. However, I know I can do only so much. You have works ahead for them to do that will require the influence of others with a more specific skill set than I possess.

I pray that my children's lives will be rich with mentors all along the way. Will You bless them with coaches, teachers, professors, pastors, and bosses who see the potential in my children and choose to pour into them? May these all be great models who are worthy of my children's respect and emulation.

May they sharpen my children not just with skills for their academic and professional lives, but also by showing them how to live with growing faith and integrity.

Amen.

Everyone must be quick to hear, slow to speak,
and slow to anger. — James 1:19

Perfect Father,

I have prayed about this verse being true in the lives of my children. I come today asking that it would be true in my life as I interact with my children.

A normal day can be filled with stress, too much to get done, and many interruptions. I confess that in the midst of being tired and stretched, I can be short-tempered.

God, please guide me and give me wisdom and patience to always listen well to my children—not to interrupt but to really pay attention, to communicate that they are worthy of my attention.

Please guide me to be slow to speak and slow to get angry. This is only possible as Your Spirit fills and leads me. Thank You that You always desire to hear Your children speak. I want to be like You. I need You today and every day.

Amen.

"There's a boy here who has five barley loaves and two
fish." ... Jesus took the loaves, and after giving thanks He
distributed them to those who were seated—so also with
the fish, as much as they wanted. — John 6:9, 11

Miracle Worker,

It is possible for You to do any work or wonder You
desire to do simply on Your own power. And yet we so
often see that You choose to work through people.

I know that my children, like everyone else, will be
painfully aware of their inadequacies. Whenever they are
aware of their lack of ability, may they recall the young
boy from today's passage. May they instead focus on Your
sufficiency.

May they never forget that You are a God of might
and miracles and can use whatever they offer to You. May
they not feel that they are ever too young (or too old), too
limited, too short on knowledge or skill. May they instead
offer You all they are and all they have and then stand
back in awe of what You can accomplish for Your glory.

Amen.

May the words of my mouth and the meditation of my heart
be acceptable to You, LORD, my rock and my Redeemer.
– Psalm 19:14

Holy One,

Today I pray for my children and for myself. May today's verse be true in our lives. May we live today knowing that nothing is unknown by You.

Every word, before we speak it, is birthed from some thought or belief within us. You know each of the meditations of our hearts. These pools within us are filled by streams, pure or impure, that we have allowed to feed into them.

May our thoughts be pure. Therefore may the words we speak be pure and holy. And guide us, Lord, that every thought and every word would be an offering to You that pleases You.

Amen.

It is a sin for the person who knows to do what is good and doesn't do it. — James 4:17

Shepherd of Our Souls,

Your Word reveals many things that to do them is to rebel against Your expressed will and to sin against You. I pray that examples of this type of disobedience will be few and far between in the lives of my children.

At other times, through Your Word and through Your Holy Spirit, You will reveal something they need to be actively doing. Like all of us, from time to time, my children will be tempted by passivity.

Today I come praying that they will reject passivity and move in obedience to do what You have called them to do. May their hearts always be tender to the promptings of Your Spirit, and may they choose to honor You through obedience.

Amen.

You, why do you criticize your brother? Or you,
why do you look down on your brother? For we will
all stand before the tribunal of God. — Romans 14:10

Righteous Judge,

You see all things and evaluate all things and all people perfectly. I pray that my children will have faith in this truth, and may they never feel the need to judge another, especially another believer.

Sometime other Christians will aggravate and frustrate my children. Especially as those who claim to bear Your name behave in ways that would seem to indicate something to the contrary, may my children know that their role is only to pray for the others and perhaps, if given the opportunity, speak the truth in tender and compassionate love.

May my children never have a harsh or self-righteous spirit.

Amen.

This is the confidence we have before Him: Whenever we ask anything according to His will, He hears us. — 1 John 5:14

God Who Hears Us,

I come today asking that my children will regularly have rich times of prayer with You. What freedom You have given us that we may ask for anything in Your name. Bless You!

I pray that my children's prayer times will not just be moments of making requests but will also be filled with worship, confession, and thanksgiving.

For all of the things they will ask of You, may they always pray as Your Son did in Gethsemane, "Not my will but Yours be done." More than things they want for themselves, may they want what You want for them.

Amen.

Therefore, if anyone is in Christ, he is a new creation; old things have passed away, and look, new things have come.
– 2 Corinthians 5:17

God Who Gives Freedom,

Every family passes down through generations some wonderful qualities and traits to their children. Every family also shares some particular weaknesses and areas of struggle.

Lord, I ask that whatever propensities toward sin I may have inherited through my family will be broken. I don't even know them all, but You do. I repent of them and ask for Your cleansing and strength to overcome.

You are almighty, powerful, and greater than any force or strength of the enemy. Will You give my children freedom from generational strongholds?

Amen.

The one who pursues righteousness and faithful love will find life, righteousness, and honor. — Proverbs 21:21

Righteous God,

I ask that my children will pursue righteousness in all of their relationships. First and foremost, may they always strive to be in right relation with You.

Then as they look around at the people they are closest to, may they look to see if all is well between them. May they take whatever steps You prompt them to take to help bring reconciliation.

Because of the way that they live—seeking after things that really matter—may there always be a rich overflow of Your blessings in their lives.

Amen.

Without wood, fire goes out; without a gossip,
conflict dies down. — Proverbs 26:20

God Who Is Truth and Loves Truth,

We all know well how it feels to pass along gossip and
how it feels to be hurt because someone else passed along
gossip about us. We know that this has no place in the lives
of Your children.

May my children reject playing the petty game of
"tearing down someone else in order to build themselves
up." May they choose, even from a young age, to stay far
away from saying things that will cause slander, strife, and
dissent.

May they instead seek to bring peace in the midst of
conflict.

Amen.

For we are His creation, created in Christ Jesus for good works, which God prepared ahead of time so that we should walk in them. – Ephesians 2:10

Master Designer,

With great joy and anticipation I think about my children's future. You have uniquely gifted and wired them for paths of service You had in mind for them from before the foundation of the world. How wild! How wonderful!

Watching the path their lives will take will be like watching a beautiful flower slowly unfold. Step-by-step, day by day Your plans and purposes will show themselves.

May You be richly blessed by the good works of my children's lives. Praise You for their perfect design.

Amen.

Act wisely toward outsiders,
making the most of the time. — Colossians 4:5

God Who Is Light,

Sometime at a young age, my children will begin to
be around nonbelievers. It may be through school, the
neighborhood, sports, and activities; but they will begin to
realize that some people have different values and beliefs
from our family.

I pray that as they grow they will be more aware of
their responsibility to be light in the darkness.

May they act toward unbelievers with authentic love
and concern. May they be wise in their behavior, find
themselves respected, and take advantage of opportunities
they have to speak truth and life. May it be always for the
glory of the gospel.

Amen.

Our mouths were filled with laughter then, and our tongues with shouts of joy. Then they said among the nations, "The LORD has done great things for them."
– Psalm 126:2

Our Dwelling Place,

God, as You reside with us within the walls of our home, I ask that joy would abound. Would You have the environment that my children grow up in (and that all of their friends might experience here) to be one of simply enjoying fellowship and time with one another?

May all who enter here feel welcome and valued. May there be a spirit of ease that is fostered through shared laughter.

May these walls resound with music that honors You. Be near us here, Lord Jesus.

Amen.

Do not be mismatched with unbelievers. For what
partnership is there between righteousness and lawlessness?
Or what fellowship does light have with darkness?
– 2 Corinthians 6:14

Holy One,

I ask many things of You regarding my children's potential spouses—that they would be loving, faithful, forgiving, respectful—but most of all I ask that they would passionately and strongly love You first and foremost. May their faith clearly be the most important part of their lives. May their love for You, Your Word, and Your people be evident.

I pray that along the way my children would not enter into a romantic or dating relationship with anyone who is not a Christian. I even ask that they would not be interested in someone of the opposite sex whose faith is new, young, or immature.

Even today, wherever their future spouses are, would You surround, protect, and bless them.

Amen.

I am Your servant; give me understanding so that
I may know Your decrees. – Psalm 119:125

Word of God,

I pray asking that at every step along the way, would
You let my children be blessed to have good Bible teachers.
From the earliest childhood classes at church, through
high school youth ministry, and even in college age groups,
may they be led by those who handle Your Word rightly.

May this simply continue to feed my children's love
for Your Word and equip them to discern the truth from
lies in conversations and in culture.

Amen.

Your life should be free from the love of money.
Be satisfied with what you have. — Hebrews 13:5

God of an Everlasting Kingdom,

Today I come to You regarding the dreams my children will dream for their future. Whatever career path they may choose, I pray that it is not driven simply by desire for financial gain.

May they look at this great world of need, have a sense of how You've gifted them, and look for the place where You might use them best for Your glory. I ask that as they serve You, would You provide for and take care of them?

May their hearts be free from the love and pursuit of material possessions.

Amen.

The fruit of the Spirit
is . . . kindness. — Galatians 5:22

Merciful One,

May my children live knowing that it takes strength to live a life of kindness. May their tender concern for friends and family show itself daily.

Though in a myriad of moments, they may want to react in anger or frustration, may they instead choose to react in a gentle manner.

Would You guide them to recognize the moments of their own pride when they are more concerned about themselves than about others? May they turn from their selfishness and find the blessing and joy that waits for those who can treat others as more important than themselves.

Amen.

No discipline seems enjoyable at the time, but painful.
Later on, however, it yields the fruit of peace and
righteousness to those who have been trained by it.
—Hebrews 12:11

Wise Shepherd,

You have certainly used what I perceived as unpleasant circumstances in my life to change my heart in ways that pleased You. Through all of my children's lives, they will face times of discipline and correction—whether from Your hand or ours or even from teachers, coaches, or bosses.

I pray that my children would maintain a tender heart and a teachable spirit.

Through the difficulties and pain of being corrected, may it indeed lead them to be wiser and more righteous as they are trained by it. May they find peace in knowing that Your heart and the heart of their parents will always be guiding them in love.

Amen.

Therefore confess your sins to one another. — James 5:16

Restorer of Unity,

Today, Lord, I am mindful that as my children grow, there may be times when I wrong them. In a moment of stress or anger, my words may be careless or hurtful. On some occasions I may misjudge a situation and wrong my children through a decision I make. It will never be my heart's desire to do this, but it will happen.

In those moments may I be quick to apologize and ask for forgiveness from my children. May they be quick to forgive.

Because You are our beautiful Redeemer, will You use even these hard times to capture my children's hearts with the beauty of humility, confession, grace, and unity?

Amen.

Ascribe to Yahweh the glory
due His name. — Psalm 29.2

Worthy One,

I pray that from a young age my children will love to worship You. I'm not asking that they simply enjoy the music and emotions that are stirred during corporate gatherings, but rather that they find delight in exalting You for being the one true God that You are. May their hearts be captured and consumed by the glory, goodness, and wonder of You.

May they worship You in times of solitude as well as in times of the body gathering.

May their worship be in spirit (the right heart attitude and passion) as well as in truth (all things consistent with what Scripture teaches).

Amen.

God is a righteous judge and a God who shows
His wrath every day. — Psalm 7:11

Perfect Judge,

One of Your attributes that we don't often consider is Your wrath. Yet it is simply another expression of Your perfection. You have a perfect fury against anything that is sin and is an offense to Your holiness. To disregard sin or to be indifferent about it would be a less than perfect response on Your part.

I pray that as my children get older and are able to begin to grasp even crumbs of this great truth, may they first and foremost be so grateful that for all who are Your children through faith, we have been delivered from Your wrath.

May this truth also lead my children to love what You love and to hate what You hate. May this spur them on to greater holiness for Your glory.

Amen.

Weeping may spend the night, but there
is joy in the morning. — Psalm 30:5

God of Every New Dawn,

My children will have to go through hard and difficult
times—times of sadness and loss, periods of testing and
trial, seasons of waiting and uncertainty—all normal dark
nights of the soul.

In these times may they keep their sight fixed on
You—trusting You, seeking You, praising You. May they
find that in Your perfect time these nights always end, and
for those who trust You, joy returns.

Even in times of sitting in shadows, may they never
lose their hope and anticipation of seeing the light of a
new day.

Amen.

Man does not see what the LORD sees, for man sees what is visible, but the LORD sees the heart. — 1 Samuel 16:7

God Who Made Us and Knows Us,

This passage today is completely and radically countercultural. We are in a world that is totally obsessed with appearance. This ever-present reminder from all media has become an incredibly destructive force in the lives of so many children and young adults.

I pray that my children will instead value what You value. May they give more care and attention to cultivating and maintaining who they are inside—character, integrity, purity, and their spiritual life.

I pray also that this is how they will assess other people—not simply on outward physical qualities but on inner qualities of virtue and integrity.

Amen.

Don't say, "I will avenge this evil!" Wait on the LORD,
and He will rescue you. — Proverbs 20:22

Our Defender,

Your care for Your children is evident moment to
moment in life. Physically and spiritually You perfectly
provide all we need.

Sometimes my children will be offended or wronged
by others. Though they may feel hurt and abandoned, may
they also feel Your nearness in those times.

May they trust that You deal perfectly with all people,
including whoever has wronged them. May they be able to
forgive, let go of the hurt, not seek revenge, and know that
You take care of Your people. The time and manner of
justice are completely up to You.

Amen.

I sought the LORD, and He answered me and delivered me from all my fears. — Psalm 34:4

Our Refuge,

At all ages, my children will encounter things that frighten them—nightmares, strangers, near accidents, as well as challenging and unusual situations.

May they learn early to call on You in those times. Though fear may grip them, it cannot hold them if they are running to You. Your power is greater than any other.

May they experience You as the God who delivers them from their fears, and may that build their faith to trust You the next time things that frighten them come around.

Amen.

A slacker's craving will kill him because
his hands refuse to work. — Proverbs 21:25

Righteous God,

A lazy child is a slow grief to You, heavenly Father,
as well as to their earthly parents. You are the God who is
always diligent, working perfectly in all things.

May my children not be lazy. May they be diligent
in housework, schoolwork, and any job they take on. If
a bent toward laziness is something they struggle with,
please guide me to instruct them carefully and wisely.

Ultimately, no matter what a parent says, only You
can change a heart. If my children continue to show a
lack of diligence, will You do what You must to turn them
from foolishness toward wisdom?

Amen.

The one who lives with integrity lives securely, but whoever perverts his ways will be found out. — Proverbs 10:9

God Who Sees and Knows All,

I pray that because of their character, my children will live with a clear conscience.

When they do sin against You or offend others, may they be quick to repent and make things right. May they live with confidence in knowing that whatever they have confessed, You have forgiven.

May there be a consistency between what they profess and the way they go about their daily lives.

Amen.

We do not want you to become lazy, but to imitate
those who through faith and patience inherit what
has been promised. – Hebrews 6:12 NIV

Great God,

You are a God of great intentionality and diligence.
You have a great plan of redemption in motion, and You
persist with that plan.

I pray that as my children make plans, large and small,
may they stick with their plans. I know that weariness and
exhaustion will set in, but please help them look to You as
the One who renews their strength.

Would You lead them to be good at persevering and
enduring in the work they take on?

Amen.

As it is, you boast in your arrogance.
All such boasting is evil. — James 4:16

Mighty Yet Meek Savior,

Pride is the seedbed for so many sins that sprout from a human heart. I pray that my children will desire and maintain a humble spirit so they avoid a world of the other sins that disrupt relationships.

If their pride goes unchecked, they could lose inner joy, peace, and confidence. They could also lose desire for drawing near to You in worship and adoration.

Instead, may they stay in right relation with You. In their humility may they be loving, gracious, and helpful as they relate with others.

Amen.

Happy is the man who fears the LORD, taking great delight in His commands. — Psalm 112:1

Living God,

Every person desires a life of heavenly blessing. Every good parent desires the same for their children.

Your Word is clear that the key to a life of blessing is reverence for You and loving obedience to Your Word. God, I ask that my children will have both of these. May they esteem You as the Most High and Holy God that You are, and may Your Word be their delight. May obedience be their first response to all You have written for them in Your Word.

As a result, may they know the life of joy, hope, and peace that comes to all who bless You.

Amen.

Everyone who will acknowledge Me before men, I will also
acknowledge him before My Father in heaven.
– Matthew 10:32

Lord,

I pray that my children will be bold in their belief.
From the time they first place their faith in You,
may there be no hesitation in letting their family, friends,
and church know about their decision, and may they also
desire to follow You in baptism.

May my children not just publicly acknowledge their
faith once . . . but often. May their words as well as their
actions clearly proclaim that You are their Savior and
Lord.

May they never deny You with their words, deeds, or
silence; but if they should have a moment of faithlessness,
may they be quick to confess their sin and find Your
forgiveness. When they do, would You lead them in
returning to a clear and strong confession of their faith?

Amen.

No one should seek his own good, but the good
of the other person.... Whether you eat or drink,
or whatever you do, do everything for God's glory.
Give no offense to the Jews or the Greeks or
the church of God. — 1 Corinthians 10:24, 31–32

God Who Gives Freedom,

As my children grow, may they be aware of their
influence on others. May they guard the integrity of their
witness.

They will face some things in life that are not
explicitly forbidden in Your Word. May my children
ask themselves whether such things are profitable and
edifying.

May they care so much for Your glory that they would
lay aside their freedom in order not to be a stumbling
block to someone else.

Amen.

Let us approach the throne of grace with boldness,
so that we may receive mercy and find grace to help
us at the proper time. — Hebrews 4:16

Our Compassionate High Priest,

Your tenderness and kindness mean so much to us.
You understand our weaknesses and our struggles. You
have felt what we feel. Bless You.

I pray that my children will find such hope and
invitation from Your compassion. May the fact that You
long for us to draw near and bring You our petitions lead
them often to call out to You.

May the faithfulness they will find from You lead
them to come before You with confidence, certain of the
grace and love they will find at Your throne.

Amen.

Do not be conformed to this age, but be transformed by the renewing of your mind, so that you may discern what is the good, pleasing, and perfect will of God. — Romans 12:2

Shepherd Who Leads Us into Purity,

I pray that my children will love You with all their mind. As a part of that, may they vigorously guard what they allow to go into their mind—what they watch, read, listen to, talk about.

May they saturate themselves with Your Word. May they love to study and meditate on Your truth.

Will You give my children a sound mind? Will You keep them from confusion and negativity? Please guard my children from any mental illnesses.

Amen.

The pure in heart are blessed,
for they will see God. – Matthew 5:8

Holy One,

You have called Your people to be holy as You are holy. We desire to, and yet we are powerless to do so without Your Spirit's help.

Just as gold is made pure from being heated and things that would contaminate it are removed, I pray that You will help my children have pure hearts before You. May their devotion to You be undivided. May they be single-minded in their love and loyalty to You.

May they turn from anything else that would try to take the attention and affection that should go to You alone.

Amen.

First, be aware of this: Scoffers will come in the last days to scoff, living according to their own desires — 2 Peter 3:3

Living God,

At some point along the way, my children will have their first encounter with someone who will academically challenge their faith. It may be in high school, college, or graduate school, but it will be a memorable and marking time.

Regardless of how my children handle it outwardly (whether they are able to be articulate in the moment or not), I care about what it does to them inwardly. In this time may they know the comfort, counsel, and encouragement of Your Spirit's presence. May it push them to be more certain of what they believe and why. I ask this knowing that as they dig deeper, they will always find You to be true and faithful.

As our Redeemer, will You please use this difficult situation in the lives of my children to bring something beautiful, powerful, useful, and glorifying to Yourself from it?

Amen.

The One who is in you is greater than
the one who is in the world. — 1 John 4:4

Almighty,

No power is like Your power. Ultimately every man,
angel, demon, and even Satan himself will bow before You
and confess that Christ is Lord!

For now we face an enemy that is real, powerful, and
active in our world. May my children have full confidence
in Your greater power. May their faith triumph over any
fear that may arise within them.

As themes and images of the kingdom of darkness
are foolishly celebrated by others in our culture, may they
hold no fear for my children. May every encounter simply
remind them that no power in the universe compares to
Yours. You are supreme and victorious.

Amen.

While Moses held up his hand, Israel prevailed, but
whenever he put his hand down, Amalek prevailed. When
Moses' hands grew heavy, they took a stone and put it under
him, and he sat down on it. Then Aaron and Hur supported
his hands, one on one side and one on the other so that his
hands remained steady until the sun went down.
– Exodus 17:11–12

Faithful,

A time will come when in the midst of serving You,
my children will need hope, encouragement, and the
company of faithful godly friends. May You guide them
always to have that kind of friend—a true one, one who
is helping to build them up and lead them into Your
blessings.

Would You help them know the sweet fellowship of
like-hearted brothers and sisters? Would You lead them
into work that will require much of their faith; yet may
they, in community with others, experience You doing
great things?

May You help my children be the kind of friends that
are a great encouragement to others, and would You have
them to experience the joy of teamwork, for Your glory,
with others?

Amen.

The Lord's slave must not quarrel,
but must be gentle to everyone. — 2 Timothy 2:24

Lamb of God,

These are days when meekness and kindness are not celebrated as virtues, and yet in Your kingdom they are prized. I pray that they will be the beautiful fruit that are born from my children's hearts of humility.

May they see all other people as Your creations and treat them with great respect. Even in the strength of their leadership of others, may there always be a spirit of tenderness.

When moments require them to be forceful and bold, may they do so without ever being harsh, overbearing, or unkind.

Amen.

Be gracious to me, God, according to Your faithful love. . . .
Wash away my guilt and cleanse me from my sin. . . .
Against You—You alone—I have sinned and done
this evil in Your sight. – Psalm 51:1–2, 4

Faithful Forgiver,

I come today asking that my children would have a tender spirit toward You when it comes to sins they commit. May they realize quickly that though they may have wronged or hurt someone else, it is ultimately You they have sinned against by failing to obey some command in Your Word.

May my children's confession to You be quick in coming, and may their cry of repentance be sincere—never just the appearance of sorrow without a true heart of turning from sin and turning toward You. May they never be stubborn or obstinate when Your spirit is prompting them.

After their cry for mercy, may they know the sweet peace of Your acceptance and be blessed by the deep joy of restoration to right relationship.

Amen.

And this is love: that we walk
according to His commands. — 2 John 6

Lord,

Throughout Your Word You make clear that to be in right relationship with You means Your people will take You at Your Word and do what You are calling them to do. This remains a constant—to love You and trust You is to obey You.

May my children's love for You be an active love, just as walking is active. May they quickly and willingly do the things You call them to do.

I ask that my children will have a deep desire to know You more, and may that draw them daily to Your Word. May they believe that their simple and pure obedience greatly honors You.

Amen.

I am the way, the truth, and the life. No one comes
to the Father except through me. — John 14:6

The Only Way,

My children will grow up in a world that sets forth
many ways to come to God. The thought of the exclusivity
of any one way will be an offense to many. However, You,
oh Savior, have the right to make the claim to be the *only
way* to God.

I pray that this will be a foundational and immovable
plank in my children's theology. May they trust in You
alone and communicate this truth clearly with every
opportunity they have.

Would You guide them to live with absolute certainty
in the wisdom of entering through the small gate and the
blessing of walking the narrow road of faith? May it be
their passion to share this truth with others.

Amen.

I am sure of this, that He who started a good work in you
will carry it on to completion until the day of Christ Jesus.
– Philippians 1:6

Faithful One,

At times along the way as my children grow, they will
reflect on life, and it may feel random and incomplete.
Facing uncertainties, difficulties, and even moments of
defeat, they might feel like their lives are wandering along
without a clear aim.

I pray that this passage will speak hope and confidence
to them. May it turn them back to Your character and give
assurance that those You call, You will justify; and those
You justify, You will glorify.

Even today, Lord, will You speak peace to my own
soul and remind me that my children are Yours and that
You have great plans for them in this life and beyond?
Bless You loving Father.

Amen.

Teach them to your children, talking about them
when you sit in your house and when you walk along the
road, when you lie down and when you get up. Write them
on the doorposts of your house and on your gates.
— Deuteronomy 11:19–20

God Who Is My God,

Your Word guides us to see that our conversations
with our children should be about You in all the common
mundane moments of life. I ask today for Your wisdom
and help to do this.

May I use every situation in life to point my children
toward You. In order to do this, I need You to change
me, to open my eyes to Your ever-present work around
me. Guide me with wisdom from Your Word that will be
appropriate for the moments of opportunity I have.

I want to take advantage of all the daily drive times,
mealtimes, bedtimes, work-around-the-house times, hang-
out and have-fun times—all of the chances to make much of
You and to be reminded of Your greatness in every moment
of our lives. May the days spent within the walls of our home
be such a time of preparation for what You have in store for
my children. Please help me do a great job in making Your
presence a part of every moment of our home life.

Amen.

I pray that you, being rooted and firmly established in love,
may be able to comprehend with all the saints what is the
length and width, height and depth of God's love, and to
know the Messiah's love that surpasses knowledge, so you
may be filled with all the fullness of God.
— Ephesians 3:17–19

Lord of Love,

I have prayed on a number of days that my children
would know without a doubt that they are loved—by You,
first and foremost, and then by myself and others.

Today I come asking that they would not only *know*
it as fact, but through Your Spirit, may they *feel* it. May
it go beyond knowledge to being an authentic experience
for them. Would You plant it deep within them that their
head and heart might join together to testify of the same
thing?

May the certainty of how loved they are give them
strength to withstand many temptations that would try to
lead them astray.

Amen.

Commit your activities to the LORD,
and your plans will be achieved. — Proverbs 16:3

Giver of the Desires of Our Heart,

It excites me when I think about the dreams and potential You have put within my children. What a thrill it will be watching these blossom and begin to unfold.

I pray that my children will always seek Your heart and Your desires for their lives. May they always ask You how You would like to use them and seek to know Your steps along the path of where life is taking them.

I pray also that any dreams they have for themselves are ones they will hold in open hands and submit to Your will. It will be a joy to behold where their righteous plans will take them as You bless and give success.

Amen.

How can they call on Him they have not believed in?
And how can they believe without hearing about Him?
And how can they hear without a preacher?
And how can they preach unless they are sent?
– Romans 10:14–15

Head of the Church,

It's clear that all who call on You for salvation are not just made saints but are also made ministers. While we live and breathe, we serve You with our lives. We build up and encourage other believers and speak the gospel to the lost.

Perhaps it will be Your plan and purpose to call my children into a church, parachurch, or missions ministry position. If so, this will be exciting, and I pray now that it would be a place that greatly uses their unique gifts and talents.

If Your design and plan for my children is a place of secular employment, I pray they will see it as their mission field and will approach the work every day envisioning themselves as one who is there to minister to those with whom they come in contact.

May they serve You with the days they have wherever they find themselves working.

Amen.

No one has greater love than this, that someone would lay down his life for his friends. — John 15:13

Our Defender and Sustainer,

I want my children to have a deep and profound gratitude for all of the courageous men and women who have bravely served to protect and help preserve our great nation.

May my children respect, honor, and express thanks to soldiers whenever they have an opportunity.

May my children only ever have the highest esteem for those who have unselfishly made incredible sacrifices to maintain our freedom.

Amen.

You will be My witnesses in Jerusalem, in all Judea and
Samaria, and to the ends of the earth. — Acts 1:8

Good News for All the World,

I pray that my children will take advantage of the
opportunities they have to witness for You. May they
passionately desire others to know of how You have saved
them, changed them, and given them a life of hope, joy,
peace, and purpose.

In all the ways they communicate with others, may
they be quick to speak of Your power and Your goodness.

May they learn how to share the gospel with others
and how to give a testimony of Your grace in their lives.
May they live with the desire for all people to know Your
good news.

Amen.

Simon, Simon, look out! Satan has asked to sift
you like wheat. But I have prayed for you that your
faith may not fail. And you, when you have turned back,
strengthen your brothers. — Luke 22:31–32

Enduring One,

I know there will be times when You allow the enemy
to test my children. They will be shaken or tempted or
tried in some way that will reveal to what extent they
are truly trusting in You. I am aware at some points my
children will give into temptations.

Though they may fail that test Lord, may their faith
never fail. When they stumble, may they be quick to
repent and desire to return to an intimate relationship
with You.

May their belief in You and their devotion to You be
proven genuine, unfailing, and enduring.

Amen.

If your brother, . . . or your closest friend secretly entices you, saying, "Let us go and worship other gods," . . . you must not yield to him or listen to him. — Deuteronomy 13:6, 8

Lord God,

I pray that as my children mature, they will be persons of great conviction. May they be strong and confident in what they believe. May their experiences in who You are give them confidence that can't be shaken even by close friends who may try to get them to compromise their beliefs.

May my children be willing to go against the flow of current culture and not be swayed by winds of popular false spiritual teaching. Would You guide them to be so confident in who You are and the perfect total authority of Your Word that they are always willing to stand for what is good and pure and loving and right?

Amen.

The highest heaven cannot
contain him.   2 Chronicles 2:6

The Ever-Present One,

You are everywhere all the time. Nothing could ever confine You. You are without limits of any kind. You reign over earth, heaven, and hell. You even enter the heart of every sinner to convict them of their sin. You are in every moment of the past. You are in every moment of the future. There is no inch of this universe or beyond that You are not fully occupying.

I pray that this marvelous truth would be a great source of comfort and hope for my children. May they know Your nearness and presence with them in every trial and temptation they face. May they find Your presence to be a great strength when they are called to be brave in serving You in some challenging way.

May Your omnipresence also motivate my children to be holy in their decisions and actions. May they realize that any moment of sin, whether in thought, word, or deed, is a moment lived out fully in Your presence.

Amen.

I am able to do all things through
Him who strengthens me. — Philippians 4:13

Our Strength,

I pray that my children will have an upbeat, positive spirit. Would You help this to come from a deep faith and confidence in who You are? May they believe they can face anything because of the boldness that comes from Your power in their lives.

Would You guide them with courage in facing trouble, pressure, temptation, and trials knowing that in Your strength they can overcome?

Your power and strength are so great and beyond anything we can imagine or dream. May the greatness of Your power be the hope and confidence that my children have in facing all things life brings. May they have a can-do spirit because they know they can do all things through You.

Amen.

Brothers, do not grow weary in doing good.
— 2 Thessalonians 3:13

The God Who Sees,

There will be times when in the midst of continuing to do the right thing, my children will see those who take advantage of the government, the church, or other agencies designed to help people. We both know how discouraging and disheartening this can be.

I pray that in these times my children will trust that You will deal rightly with all offenders in the perfect time. May my children choose to continue doing what is right. Would You send reminders to them in their discouragement that You know all, see all, and always act justly?

May this bring them renewed strength.

Amen.

Grace was given to each one of us according
to the measure of the Messiah's gift. – Ephesians 4:7

Equipper of the Saints,

Lord, I trust that You have uniquely gifted my children to serve You and Your church. I pray that You would guide me to help my children develop their gifts. Would You show me where some special nurturing might be required? Would You let me see any place where lessons or training could help develop their gifts?

I ask that even today You may be revealing to my children what their talents are. Somehow, through the work of Your Holy Spirit, may my children learn what their gifting is. Though it could change through the years, may they be on the path of following Your lead.

May they know Your voice, Your call, and not spend large seasons of their lives trying to figure out where You are leading. Please protect their gifting that it may not be used for a lesser purpose than what You desire. May their lives always be for Your glory.

Amen.

It is also the gift of God whenever anyone eats, drinks, and enjoys all his efforts. — Ecclesiastes 3:13

One Who Gives Life Meaning.

I pray that You will direct my children to work that is meaningful to them and honoring to You.

Even from a young age, will You put within them an enjoyment of some activities that give them deep satisfaction? Would You use these interests along with wise and godly counsel from Your Word to point a general direction for the path my children's lives should take? Even if throughout their lives they change jobs a number of times, may it be going from one thing that gives them joy to something that gives them greater joy. May they be grateful for the work You lead them to and find satisfaction in doing it with excellence.

I pray that they will bless You as the One who has led them into meaningful and purposeful labor.

Amen.

We must not get tired of doing good, for we will reap at the proper time if we don't give up. — Galatians 6:9

Persistent Faithful One,

You have ordained good works for all of Your children to do. Some may be short-term works, and others will be those that continue over the duration of a lifetime. I pray that my children will be committed to completing all tasks You have for them with excellence.

May they stay focused on You, and may You renew their strength when they grow weary.

Though a job may go on and on, with no end in sight, may my children not truly consider giving up. May they instead know the blessing and reward You have for those who persist in doing good—eternal rewards as well as blessings in the here and now.

Amen.

Then the LORD God said, "It is not good for the man to be alone. I will make a helper as his complement." . . . This is why a man leaves his father and mother and bonds with his wife, and they become one flesh. — Genesis 2:18, 24

Giver of the Gift of Marriage,

I pray that of all the many influences that have an effect on my children's view of marriage, none would speak louder or be more cherished than Your Holy Word. May my children truly trust that only the One who designed and gifted us with marriage can adequately speak of what marriage should look like.

Should there come a time when after seeking Your heart and will, my children believe they have found the one You would have them marry, may they both spend time going deep in Your Word to see the riches of all You have to say about love, commitment, submission, and purity.

If marriage is in Your will for my children, may this be an area of life where they find great joy and the richest blessings from Your hand.

Amen.

Praise the God and Father of our Lord Jesus Christ,
the Father of mercies and the God of all comfort. He
comforts us in all our affliction, so that we may be able
to comfort those who are in any kind of affliction,
through the comfort we ourselves receive from God.
– 2 Corinthians 1:3–4

Our Comforter,

There will be some dark days and hard times that
You lead my children into and then lead them through. In
the midst of it, I pray that they will know Your closeness
and Your comfort.

You are such a Redeemer. You take the difficult
things we face and actually bring good from them. Bless
You.

May the precious truths my children will learn
about You as You comfort them be the truths they will
one day turn around and share with others facing similar
situations.

Amen.

Giving thanks always for everything to God the Father
in the name of our Lord Jesus Christ. — Ephesians 5:20

Gracious God,

I ask today that my children would always have a
spirit of thanksgiving. May they be constantly aware that
every good thing in their lives has come from You. Every
friendship, every blessing, every blue sky, and even every
heartbeat are gifts from You.

May they never have a spirit of entitlement or a
haughty thought of deserving more, but may they live with
a daily awareness of Your lavish provision.

May their gratitude find regular expression in their
words about You and in their prayers to You.

Amen.

You must keep My Sabbaths and revere My sanctuary;
I am Yahweh. – Leviticus 19:30

Holy King,

I pray that my children will live with a deep reverence
of You. May they esteem and honor Your name and never
consider misspeaking or misusing it in a way that is
dishonoring to You.

I pray that they will have great respect for Your Book
and will never treat it lightly or mishandle it. May they
revere every day of the week as a holy gift You have given;
yet may they respect Sunday as an ordained day of rest.

May they have respect for the building where Your
people gather to worship as well as for all of the men and
women who serve You in ministry.

Amen.

The fruit of the Spirit
is . . . patience. – Galatians 5:22

God Who Is Slow to Anger,

In the midst of a society that desires everything instantly, we stand with a slow and steady calmness. We are sure who You are. We are sure that every promise in Your Word will be perfectly fulfilled. Therefore, we can rest.

I know my children will have frustrations with their limitations at some point in their lives and will become irritated. They may even have to endure some painful seasons that seem to go on for an unreasonable length of time.

May they patiently endure. May they not grow weary but calmly accept where You have them. May they patiently serve You through all of life and trust You for the results.

Amen.

Whatever is true, whatever is honorable, whatever is just, whatever is pure, whatever is lovely, whatever is commendable—if there is any moral excellence and if there is any praise—dwell on these things. — Philippians 4:8

Holy One,

I pray that my children will take seriously Your command to guard their minds. Whatever they allow into their minds will surely find an expression in their words and actions.

May they be so diligent and so wise in the forms of media they allow before their eyes, ears, and into their thoughts. May they, with great intentionality, gravitate toward things that are respectable, pure, right, and God honoring.

Would You allow this to lead to excellence and fruitfulness in serving You as well as good mental and psychological health for them?

Amen.

If either falls, his companion can lift him up; but pity the
one who falls without another to lift him up.
— Ecclesiastes 4:10

Our Faithful Friend,

You did not create us for isolation but that we may
know life in community and in intimacy. I pray that
my children will always have a good number of true
companions in life, the kind who encourage them and
keep them strong in their faith.

Some darker and more difficult moments will surely
come in my children's stories. Perhaps even times when
they stumble. I pray there will be significant people in
their lives to help them back on their feet and back onto
the pathways. May they be blessed by the faithfulness of
their friends.

And in return may my children be there to help
restore and encourage their friends in their hour of
need. May a life of isolation never hold an appeal for my
children.

Amen.

Now to Him who is able to do above and beyond all that
we ask or think according to the power that works in us.
– Ephesians 3:20

Almighty One,

On many days and in many ways, I have prayed for
my children to have faith. I come today to ask that they
will not simply have a faith that trusts in You but a faith
that will come before You and pray for incredible things in
Your name for Your glory. I ask that my children will be so
convinced of Your almighty power and that miracles are
possible that they dare to pray for You to do great things
that only You can do.

May they ask for You to heal. May they ask for You to
make a way where there is no way. May they pray for You
to change a heart—all works that only You can do.

Would You allow my children to have great
confidence that with You all things are possible and
nothing is impossible?

Amen.

When He saw the crowds, He felt compassion
for them, because they were weary and worn out,
like sheep without a shepherd. – Matthew 9:36

Searching Shepherd,

Sometimes in my children's lives those who don't
trust in You will cause them great anger and frustration.
In those moments will You meet my children with the
insight that these people are simply behaving in ways that
are consistent with their unredeemed nature?

May my children's spirit be tender toward them and
moved with compassion for them.

May my children always have a sensitivity to and a
heart for those who don't know You yet. May they see
them as ultimately searching for meaning, truth, and You.

Amen.

Dear friends, if God loved us in this way,
we also must love one another. – 1 John 4:11

Loving Father,

Your great love for us is expressed in so many ways
that it is beyond our ability even to imagine them all. Yet
none is clearer than in the giving of Your only Son.

I pray for my children, as for all believers, that Your
sacrificial love on Calvary is the redefining moment of
their lifetime.

I ask that my children's love for others will be
expressed through their willing sacrifice of their desires,
wants, and rights for the good of others. May friends see
in my children the absence of pride that frees them to
truly love as a reflection of Your love.

Amen.

No foul language is to come from your mouth,
but only what is good for building up someone in need,
so that it gives grace to those who hear. – Ephesians 4:29

Word of Life,

I have prayed about the words I wish not to come from the lips of my children. Today, Lord, I come asking that they will be quick to speak Your Word to others.

Would You gift my children with the ability to recall the right verse for the right moment? Those who do this well so often have such a powerful and holy influence as they go through life.

Would You help my children memorize and truly hide Your Word in their hearts that they may beautifully overflow to build up and encourage others?

Amen.

The one who lives with integrity is righteous; his children who come after him will be happy. – Proverbs 20:7

Holy One,

It is my prayer and heart's deep desire to be holy as You are, as You have called me to be.

It is a sobering thing to realize that when it comes to my children and their faith, so much more will be *caught* from me than *taught*.

God, I want to live a life that sets an example of one who is in passionate pursuit of Your heart and mind. I want my life to show a love of Your Word, worship that is filled with spirit and truth, joyful service to those of the church and those of the world.

Remind me today that my actions have consequences. May I never do anything that might be a stumbling block to my children's faith.

I declare my ongoing need for Your daily grace, wisdom, and strength. Will You help my children follow me as You help me to follow You?

Amen.

Do not cause anyone to stumble.
– 1 Corinthians 10:32 NIV

Holy One,

There will be people my children respect and look up to spiritually. I pray that these people will know the important role they play in the life of younger believers and will avoid compromise and failure that could be so devastating to themselves, others, and my children.

Likewise, I pray that my children's actions will never be a stumbling block to someone else. May nothing they say or do be a hindrance for a nonbeliever coming to You.

May my children be willing to set aside their liberty if it could possibly cause a weaker believer to stumble.

Amen.

Your decrees are my delight and my counselors.
— Psalm 119:24

Wonderful Counselor,

My children will have many people speaking into their lives—parents, extended family, neighbors, friends of the family, ministers, teachers, coaches, guidance counselors . . . in addition to all they will absorb through media.

Many will even give good advice, but may there be none they depend on or trust in like they trust in Your Word.

Your wisdom surpasses even the best and highest thoughts of any person.

Amen.

Those who are persecuted for righteousness are blessed,
for the kingdom of heaven is theirs. — Matthew 5:10

Jesus the Crucified,

I'm aware that if my children should live as I have been praying they will, at points along the way their righteousness will be an offense to others. It may be because of a refusal to cheat or join others in a compromise; it may be because of some truth they have spoken, but somehow at some point others will dislike them.

They may know people speaking ill of them behind their back or even directly. They may face some direct physical confrontation. Will You meet them in those times? Will You protect them? Will You give them strength, comfort, and peace to endure and stand strong?

May any resistance not discourage them but in fact encourage them that the life they are living is one that honors You. Please guide, bless, and take care of my children.

Amen.

I will both lie down and sleep in peace, for You alone,
LORD, make me live in safety. – Psalm 4:8

Prince of Peace,

I lift up to You the times my children will spend in their room. May all the things they do in there—read, play, daydream, listen to music, schoolwork, time with friends—be honoring to You.

I invite You to be Lord over all conversations that will happen between the walls. Please keep them from wrong and dishonoring topics, and keep them focused on what is holy and pure. May that room be a safe, peaceful place for my children to grow into who You are making them to be.

May they be able to lie down and sleep in peace at the end of every day with the work and concerns of the day attended to and set aside. Please guide their thoughts as they lie awake and look back on their day and as they look ahead in anticipation. Please meet and lead them in those moments.

Amen.

"Everything is permissible for me," but not everything is helpful. "Everything is permissible for me," but I will not be brought under the control of anything. – 1 Corinthians 6:12

God of Freedom,

We live in a day of excess. Even with many things that are good in moderation, there are always those who will take them to extreme amounts. Spiritual bondage is most often the result of this.

I pray that my children will submit their desires and passions to You inviting You to be Lord over those (and all) areas of their lives. May they be cautiously mindful of even letting small patterns develop into enslaving habits in their lives.

May they walk in freedom with You.

Amen.

Christ in you, the hope of glory. – Colossians 1:27

Our Unfailing Hope,

What a marvelous, incomprehensible truth that You would choose to dwell within Your children. What a secure and unshakable foundation for our hope to be built upon. Any of this world who put their hope in anyone or anything else will ultimately be disappointed.

I pray that hope will always be strong and vibrant within my children. Even as they face times of being frustrated and disheartened, may they clearly know that You have good things ahead for them. May this hope be an anchor that keeps them from drifting into discouragement and depression.

May Your Word and their worship always stir the flame of hope within them.

Amen.

Do not despise the LORD's instruction, my son, and do not loathe His discipline; for the LORD disciplines the one He loves, just as a father, the son he delights in.
— Proverbs 3:11–12

Perfect Father,

There will be times when, as my children grow, they will be subject to Your discipline in order to correct and instruct them. This may include times of suffering and consequences.

I pray that my children will be quick in responding to You by crying out to know what the lesson is for them.

Even in the midst of the most difficult days, may they never question whether You love them. May they be certain of that and truly believe You are perfect in all Your ways. May they see that You always lead us along in paths that will grow our faith and increase our wisdom and blessings.

May Your discipline in their lives produce much fruit for Your honor. Please guide them to endure well.

Amen.

And Jesus increased in wisdom. — Luke 2:52

Wise One,

I pray that my children would be blessed with a deep desire to learn. Would You give them a sharp mind and a diligent spirit to seek after wisdom?

Would the process of reading and hearing instruction be joyful to my children. May they not be lazy but motivated to press on with their education.

More than simply gaining knowledge, may they have a deep hunger for the eternal truths of Your Word.

Amen.

The fruit of the Spirit
is . . . peace.   Galatians 5:22

Prince of Peace,

Simply knowing You produces peace in the hearts of Your children. What a calming truth when we rest in the fact that the Almighty King and Creator of the universe has accepted us through our faith in the sacrificial death of His Son.

Our peace rests in Your character. May this be the foundation of peace in my children's lives. May they be so confident in Your Sovereignty over all events of their lives that even in the midst of storms, their spirit knows that all is well.

May this peace conquer all of their fears and doubts.

Amen.

God's love was revealed among us in this way:
God sent His One and Only Son into the world so
that we might live through Him. – 1 John 4:9

God Who Is Love,

Your love is expressed to us in hundreds of ways every moment. Of the countless ways we know we are loved by You, there is none greater than the fact that You sent Your Son to be our Savior.

This time of the year, when the sights and sounds of the holiday bombard us from all angles, I pray that the primary message my children think about as they experience the season is . . . YOU LOVE THEM.

May everything about this holiday bring to their minds that You initiated toward them, You pursued them, You desire relationship with them, and You made a way for them to have relationship with You. We are amazed.

Amen.

The one who loves a pure heart and gracious lips—
the king is his friend. ~ Proverbs 22.11

God of Truth and Wisdom,

You make clear to us that our lips simply give expression to what is already within us. I pray that pure love, worship, grace, and wisdom will overflow from my children.

As a result, may they have amazing and redemptive influence with people. Would You use them powerfully in the lives of others that they are around day to day, and at times would You grant them access, favor, and even influence on those who have a great influence on many others?

Amen.

Be on guard against all greed because one's life is not
in the abundance of his possessions. -- Luke 12:15

God of Heavenly Riches,

The seeds of desiring more material possessions are
sown into the fabric of every TV, magazine, and radio
advertisement we encounter. A result of simply, casually
walking in the mall and window-shopping is that we
become discontent with what we already have and want
something new instead.

Lord, I know that the spirit of materialism will try
to get its hooks in my children, but I pray asking that
You would thwart this. May my children live in freedom.
Will You guide them never to be caught in a pattern
of coveting? May they not put great value in things but
instead see that real riches are found in relationships.

When they have a choice between striving for
spiritual blessing and material blessing, may they choose
what really satisfies and endures.

Amen.

> We know that all things work together for
> the good of those who love God: those who are
> called according to His purpose. — Romans 8:28

Sovereign King,

I pray that the promise of today's verse will bring glorious and holy hope to the hearts of my children. May they come to have great confidence that although not all things that happen in life are good, still for Your people You work in the midst of all things to accomplish Your glory and their ultimate good.

In some of the darker and harder times of their lives—suffering, temptation, loss, sin, failure, heartbreak, disappointment—may the truth of Your sovereignty be a precious pearl my children will cling to and find in it great hope, comfort, and encouragement.

Amen.

Children, obey your parents in everything,
for this pleases the Lord. – Colossians 3:20

Our Perfect Father,

You do not delight in outward conformity that happens apart from a heart that is set on doing what is right. It is much like a defiant child who finally obeys a parent's instruction. The child reluctantly sits down, exclaiming, "I'm sitting down in the chair, but in my heart I'm still standing!"

May this spirit of rebellion and pride not exist in my children. Lord, if any seeds of pride fall upon my children's hearts, may they simply not find soil to grow in. May my children willingly comply with instruction from sweet, submissive, and fully trusting hearts.

May this attitude of love, trust, and honor characterize my children's relationship with me for all of our days.

Amen.

Let your word "yes" be "yes," and your "no" be "no."
Anything more than this is from the evil one.
– Matthew 5:37

Righteous Judge,

I pray that my children's integrity will speak such volumes that in many moments their words can be few. May their routine conversation time after time be proven to be honest and right.

May their reputation be so sterling that they would never need to resort to swearing to convince someone of their integrity.

Amen.

Don't neglect to do what is good and to share, for God is
pleased with such sacrifices. – Hebrews 13:16

Our Generous God,

I ask that my children would believe that every
good thing they have been given comes as a gift from
You. Therefore, may they learn to hold loosely to all
possessions, trusting that the One who gave in the first
place can always give more.

May my children reflect Your generous heart in the
way they handle things that belong to them. May they be
unselfish and willing to share.

I ask this particularly as it relates in their relationships
with siblings.

Amen.

This Jesus, who has been taken from you into heaven,
will come in the same way that you have seen
Him going into heaven. — Acts 1:11

God Who Is Faithful to Return,

This season of the year is such a time of anticipation,
especially for children. They can't wait to get out of
school, take part in holiday traditions, and most of all
open presents!

We sing songs that reflect our longing to see You in
Your incarnation: "O Come, O Come Emmanuel" and
"Come Thou Long-Expected Jesus."

I pray that my children will always live with a sweet
anticipation of Your return to earth. May they live with
a sure faith and confidence that You are faithful to Your
promise to return again—this time not as a humble baby
but as the reigning mighty King of kings and Lord of lords.

Amen.

Like newborn infants, desire the pure spiritual milk,
so that you may grow by it. — 1 Peter 2:2

God Who Leads Us Onward,

I pray that my children would have an enormous
appetite for knowing Your Word. May their love for and
delight in Your truth be evident to any around them.

I pray that this would be a relentless passion
throughout every season of their lives. May they always
put themselves in situations to receive the most excellent
true teaching available. Would You guide them in finding
great Bible-believing churches and ministries that can
help them grow?

May they never be satisfied with lite topical talks
about spiritual things but always crave the meat and
meaning of every word of Your holy truth.

Amen.

Each person should do as he has decided in his heart—not reluctantly or out of necessity, for God loves a cheerful giver.
— 2 Corinthians 9:7

Lavish Giver of Grace and Every Blessing,

You know that my desire is for my children to live with open hands, not clutching or clinging to anything You have given them but being willing to pass it on as a blessing to others.

May my children live with hearts that find it a joyous privilege to give to You. I ask that at times their giving would be spontaneous, but more importantly may it always be planned and systematic . . . and never grudgingly or sporadic.

May they always know the incredible richness of being a channel of Your blessings.

Amen.

See, the virgin will become pregnant and give birth
to a son, and they will name Him Immanuel,
which is translated "God is with us." – Matthew 1:23

Our Ever-Present Savior,

I ask that Your name Immanuel will deeply impact
the life of my children.

May they:

always be in wonder that You initiated and
came to earth to redeem us;

find great comfort in Your presence during
the most difficult, sad, frightening times of their
lives;

know the peace found in Your nearness in
times of failure;

experience courage knowing You are with
them as they step into the unknown;

find Your closeness to be a charge to sober
living as they face times of temptation.

We bless You Jesus for being with us!!

Amen.

Rejoice in the Lord always. I will say it again.
Rejoice! — Philippians 4:4

God of Joy,

Since Your Word repeatedly commands us to be joyful, our assumption is that You understand well that it is not always easy to be joyful. Joy must be more than an emotion, for You wouldn't command us to feel a feeling!

I pray that my children will know deep constant joy—the confidence that You are in control of everything and are working for their good and Your glory. May this truth produce within their souls an abiding sense of peace and hopefulness that no circumstance can shake.

May this be the true joy that fills them.

Amen.

Giving thanks always for everything to God the Father
in the name of our Lord Jesus Christ. – Ephesians 5:20

Gift of God,

I ask that my children's hearts would be a garden of
gratitude where so many other virtues may grow and bear
fruit. May my children be thankful for every gift, blessing,
and good thing that comes their way.

I pray also that they will do what's even harder to
do—be thankful for blessings and victories that are yet
to come. At times when they feel stuck and are waiting
for You to move, may their confidence in Your goodness
cause them to express their gratitude to You in advance as
they anticipate Your answer to their prayers.

As my children grow, Lord, I pray that they may
even be able to do that which is hardest to do—express
thankfulness to You in the midst of pain, trial, persecution,
or a time of testing. This can only come from a heart that
is consumed with the glory of who You are.

I want that for my children.

Amen.

Today a Savior, who is Messiah the Lord,
was born for you in the city of David. — Luke 2:11

Most High God,

Thank You for this blessed day of celebration!

This day, and the season that surrounds it, becomes
filled with so many things, and many of these are even
good things. I pray that our family will find creative ways
to keep our hearts focused on the heart of this holiday.

You saw our great need. You solved our greatest
problem. You provided for us what we were helpless to
provide for ourselves.

You sent us a Savior!

May my children, and our whole family, express our
gratitude and bless You today for Your Gift to us.

Amen.

Do nothing out of rivalry or conceit, but in humility
consider others as more important than yourselves.
– Philippians 2:3

Servant of God,

It is easy to have angry words and aggressive actions
going between two proud people, but between two
humble people it's almost impossible.

I pray today that my children will truly, in a healthy,
holy way, consider the needs of others as more important
than their own. This, to me, seems the heart of helping
my children live lives that overcome selfishness, pride,
and conceit—all the things that will cause conflict in their
relationship with You, me, and everyone else.

Today I pray particularly that this humble selflessness
will show itself strongly in relationships with siblings. May
we have a home where thoughtfulness, kindness, concern,
sharing, and love are lived out daily. What a delightful,
heavenly life that would be! Please help us.

Amen.

Forgetting what is behind and reaching forward
to what is ahead, I pursue as my goal the prize promised
by God's heavenly call in Christ Jesus. — Philippians 3:13–14

God of Our Tomorrows,

I pray that my children will always live as those whose eyes are fixed on what's ahead. May they be so certain that Your mercy and grace have covered any and all past mistakes that they are never bound or hindered by grudges, bitterness, failures, or missed opportunities of the past.

May they also never run as those who are looking back over their shoulders even when it comes to successes. Would You not let them focus on achievements, virtuous deeds, or accomplishments of the past but see them simply as offerings already laid at Your feet?

May they never see themselves as defined by past victories or past failures.

Amen.

I have no greater joy than this: to hear that my children
are walking in the truth. – 3 John 4

Living God,

I have prayed often this year about the place of
importance I would like Your Word to occupy in the lives
of my children. I pray about this so much because I truly
believe it is the pathway to salvation for them.

I want them to love, believe, and obey Your Word—
not just now and not just simply for a long season of their
life. No, I ask that this would be the true and enduring
pattern for the length of their lifetimes.

For Your great glory, now and forever more.

Amen.

He leads me along the right paths
for His name's sake. — Psalm 23:3

Shepherd,

It is easy to trust You with my children. You are
perfect in all Your ways. Your love for each of us, including
my children, is incomprehensible. You are faithful to
provide, protect, and care for each of Your children.

As my children look to the seasons of life and years
ahead, may they have confidence in Your active leading
hand upon them. This is my peace—that if they are
seeking You and You are leading them, I know You are
leading them in paths of righteousness.

This will be my great joy to watch Your plan, purpose,
and pathway unfold for their lives.

Amen.

I prayed for this child, and the LORD has granted me what
I asked of him. So now I give him to the LORD. For his
whole life he will be given over to the LORD.
– 1 Samuel 1:27–28 NIV

Gracious Giver,

Even now I can recall the overwhelming joy of the
first time I held my children—life-changing gifts from
You. For all of the incredible joyous moments of being a
parent, there will also be some really difficult ones. Many
of those will have to do with moments of letting go. Some
are small, and others are large and nearly heartrending.

All along the way there will be many moments of letting
go, and they will all call for me to trust You. Whether it's the
first time with a babysitter, first day of kindergarten or high
school, out-of-town trips, mission trips, college, or ultimately
marriage, these moments will stir intense emotions.

Yet through it all, I will look to You and rest in
knowing that You love my children even more than I do.
Your love is deeper, higher, wider, more lasting, and more
perfect. You are fully able to protect and keep them safe in
Your hand. My peace is in Your sovereignty. I will rest in
who You are. Help me be one who releases well.

Thank You for Your great love for my children.

Amen.

From eternity to eternity the LORD's faithful love is toward those who fear Him, and His righteousness toward the grandchildren of those who keep His covenant, who remember to observe His precepts. – Psalm 103:17–18

Father,

I come to You today at the end of the year in a time that for many is reflective and for others is about looking ahead. I find myself doing both. I am so aware of Your goodness and mercy leading up to this moment in my family tree. You have pursued me, called me to Yourself, and granted me faith to trust in You.

I know You also have great plans for my children and have heard me pour out my petitions on their behalf.

With all of the good, right, and holy things I desire for them, I also want these same things for their children's children . . . should You so choose to bless them in this way. I want us to be a part of a legacy that brings great glory to You for being the Redeemer that You are. I want the generations that follow in our family to know Your love and to walk closely with You.

That You might be glorified, forever!

Amen.

INDEX

ABOUT THE AUTHOR

TONY WOOD is a multiple Gospel Music Association Dove Award winner as well as nominee for Songwriter of the Year. He has written songs recorded by: Michael W. Smith, Point of Grace, Francesca Battistelli, Matt Redman, 4-HIM, Mandisa, Jason Crabb, Sandi Patty, Kutless, Natalie Grant, Mark Harris, Larnelle Harris, SELAH, Group 1 Crew, Gaither Vocal Band, Steven Curtis Chapman, Mark Schultz, Booth Brothers, Kari Jobe, Chris August, Oak Ridge Boys, and many others. He and his wife Terri are the parents of four daughters. This is his first book.

www.tonywoodonline.com

twitter.com/tonywood_exit71